The Essential Buyer's Guide

VOLKSWAGEN

T4

Transporter, Caravelle and Camper models,
1990 to 2003

Your marque experts:
Ken Cservenka & Richard Copping

VELOCE PUBLISHING
THE PUBLISHER OF FINE AUTOMOTIVE BOOKS

www.veloce.co.uk

EARTHWORLD EXPANDING HORIZONS

Hubble & Hattie   Hubble & Hattie

First published March 2020 by Veloce Publishing Limited, Veloce House, Parkway Farm Business Park, Middle Farm Way, Poundbury, Dorchester DT1 3AR, England. Fax 01305 268864 / e-mail info@veloce.co.uk / web www.veloce.co.uk or www.velocebooks.com.
ISBN 978-1-787114-38-8 / UPC 6-36847-01438-4

We have a suspicion that either you know your T4s and are specifically looking for a given model, or you want a Camper and have heard that a VW is your best bet.

In the case of the former and without detriment to the latter, we've both been around VWs for a long time and think we can suggest what's best and what's not quite so good – even if it seems like a good idea. We'll detail the years when the T4 was produced, and when those we consider to be the models that tick all the boxes were introduced. Inevitably, we'll concentrate on those VWs we've seen that are either standard, or closer to original spec than the fully-customised offerings. On the other hand, we'll also point out what's good and bad to look for if your dream is someone else's bespoke creation.

This long-nose Caravelle was clearly bought for its luxury specification and ability to carry a large family of passengers.

If your goal is ownership of a VW Camper, hopefully we can guide you towards the *crème de la crème*, both in terms of base models and conversion companies, not to mention the enormous coach-built bodies gently lowered onto a chassis cab. We'll tell you why a T4 is more practical than even its immediate predecessor, and certainly why – lovely though they are – the split-screen and bay-window can't offer what a T4 can. We'll also discuss many an enthusiast's view that a good T4 is a much better buy than its successor, the T5. We'll hover around home-spun conversions at least briefly, too.

Beware, however, of VW's reputation as being a cut above many of its competitors in terms of build quality and reliability, and of its proven Camper

The freedom of a home on wheels in T4 guise attracts many buyers. This example illustrates the shorter front that was available when the T4 launched.

It's not totally unrealistic to purchase a T4 for your business needs. VW T4s have long lives.

heritage dating right back to the 1950s. The T4's popularity as an offshoot of both means that you'll pay more than you would for an equivalent model of a similar age from another manufacturer. We think a good T4 is worth every penny (if you've followed our guidelines), but you might think we are biased.

Briefly, just to make sure we are on the same wavelength: the T4 was introduced in 1990 and was replaced by the T5 13 years later, in 2003. It could be purchased from VW as a Delivery Van and in other workhorse guises (including a chassis cab or pick-up), or as a Caravelle. This term means 'people carrier,' and invariably a posh one at that. VW didn't manufacture a Camper before the arrival of the T5. Instead they supplied bodies to others, some of which enjoyed partnerships or approved statuses.

Finally, a word or two about our credentials – one of us has written a book about the T4 from its inception to the day the final example rolled off VW's assembly line. The other loves oil and grease, as his book about VW engines testifies. One of us is a regular contributor to the leading *VW Camper* magazine in Britain, while the other has spent hours compiling what the T4's biggest assets are and when, if ever, it's likely to go wrong.

Contents

1 Is it the right car for you?
– marriage guidance

Tall and short drivers
Suited to all shapes and sizes of owner – the driver's seat is adjustable for height and rake whatever the model.

Weight of controls
Earlier T4s lacked power steering and had disc brakes at the front only. Discs all-round became universal in 1996.

Will it fit in the garage?
The biggest – a LWB, long-nose, new profile bumper model (post 1996) – measures 5189mm. The shortest – a SWB, old bumper model – measures 4655mm. Maximum width never exceeds 2175mm. Overall standard height is 1940mm (though coachbuilt Campers could vary).

Maximum interior space
In Delivery Van guise; SWB: 5.4 cubic metres, LWB: 6.3 cubic metres.

Running costs
The most economical of the diesels – the 2.5TDI 102PS – offers 34.9 mpg in an urban cycle, while the 2.8-litre VR6 petrol engine's urban cycle results in 18.6 mpg.

Usability
Practical for daily all-year usage.

Parts availability
Both genuine VW and aftermarket parts are readily available.

Parts cost
Genuine VW parts tend to be pricey; aftermarket alternatives are cheaper, but are they comparable?

Insurance group
Standard cover with restricted mileage won't be too bad. Campers need contents insurance, but may be cheaper than a van in daily use. Customised vans with re-mapped engines pay a penalty. Agreed value insurance is probably the best bet.

Investment potential
The T4, particularly the long-nose models, are probably a safer bet than the T5 and especially the T6. Splits and Bays command the highest prices, while some regard the T3 with distaste, which affects values. In straight investment terms, a T4 Camper isn't going to make you a mint, but won't depreciate much, if at all.

Foibles
Very high mileage and a lack of care and attention are the biggest issues, but specific foibles are singular by their absence.

This attractive and still modern-looking cab illustrates the comfort of owning a Volkswagen T4.

Plus points
Modern in concept, and makes a great Camper; the 2.5TDI is long-lived and relatively economical; popular; has a reputation of being more reliable than a T5; aesthetically more pleasing than a T3; few rust buckets.

Minus points
Lacks the charisma of Splits and Bays; oldest examples are getting long in the tooth and can be thirsty; pricey on occasion – you are paying for the VW name.

Alternatives
If you want to be a member of the VW fraternity there's no alternative other than older or newer models. If not, think Ford, Vauxhall, French and Japanese models.

2 Cost considerations
– affordable, or a money pit?

The manufacturer recommends an oil change service interval of every 10,000 miles – or 15,000km – or once a year, minimum, for most lubrication and adjustment cycles. A change of cambelt and injection pump drivebelt (2.5TDI only) is recommended at every 80,000 miles or 120,000km. Brake fluid should be changed every two years.

VW parts are never the cheapest, although chances of calling out the AA are reassuringly low.

Small service ●x100 from independent VW specialist
Large service ●x250 from independent VW specialist
New clutch from ●x110 (not fitted)
New clutch and flywheel kit, 2.5TDI ACV Engine ●x550
Rebuilt engine
　　Four-cylinder 1.9TDI ●x2000
　　Five-cylinder 2.4TDI ●x2500 to ●x3600, depending on engine code.
　　Five-cylinder 2.5TDI from ●x3000, depending on engine code.
Turbocharger ●x460
1.9 cylinder head from ●x550 (each, not fitted)
2.5 cylinder head from ●x690 (each, not fitted)
Change cambelt and water pump from ●x320

Brake disc, front ●x35
Brake disc, rear ●x35
Brake drum, rear ●x50. Pre-May 1996 models only.

Brake pads, front and rear from ⬤x30
Brake shoes, rear ⬤x35
Brake callipers, front ⬤x80
Brake callipers, rear ⬤x65
Brake servo from ⬤x95
Steering rack from ⬤x180
Rear coil springs from ⬤x50
Set of four shock absorbers from ⬤x175
Outer CV joint from ⬤x45
Inner CV joint from ⬤x55
New headlight, original equipment ⬤x150
Catalytic converter 1992-1995 from ⬤x180
Exhaust System from ⬤x110 (not fitted)
Exhaust downpipe, 1.9TDI 1990-1995 ⬤x65
Front bumper from ⬤x65
Rear bumper from ⬤x85
Full respray from ⬤x4000 (including preparation)
Full professional restoration of a T4 in poor condition from ⬤x6000

Parts that are easy to find
Service items and most engine parts.

Parts that are hard to find
Original VW Body panels, and instrument panels.

Parts that are very expensive
Flywheel and clutch kits for a 2.5TDI ACV code engine.

3 Living with a T4
– will you get along together?

First of all, is a T4 suitable as a daily driver? Most might consider an example built in the early '90s a little elderly for such a role, but certainly – at the time of publication – to see a later T4 performing duties as a school bus, or acting as a workhorse for butcher, baker or builder is not out of the ordinary. If it's a diesel, even with in excess of 100,000 miles on the clock, there are many, many thousands of miles left in it.

Of course, at least half of you are not in the market for a T4 as a daily driver. You are looking for a Camper, a vehicle likely to be used during an extended summer period (probably stretching from Easter to the end of November), at weekends and for holidays. Considering we would argue that a VW Camper 30 years older than the most elderly T4 is okay for such purposes, we would say VW's fourth generation model is ideal for you.

Although larger than the average car, even in long-wheelbase guise the T4 isn't so enormous that garaging it is nigh-on impossible (there is an exception, and that's the coach-built body models mounted on a chassis cab, but few would even contemplate trying to squeeze such a vehicle into a domestic garage). We'd suggest that a vehicle likely to be off the road in the depths of winter should enjoy the comforts of a dry garage or a car-port – and, yes, many enthusiasts build one or the other in a manner designed to cope with fixed high roofs, or the added centimetres of an elevating roof.

The T4 was the first VW Transporter to feature short- and long-wheelbase options. Here's an LWB option with plenty of legroom.

A lovely T4 short-wheelbase Delivery Van, ripe for use as it was built, or for conversion into a Camper.

Rust-proofing treatment had moved on in leaps and bounds from the days of the T4's predecessor. Key was the notion that treatment was applied during manufacture and encompassed internal body sections and panels. Post '96, and the introduction of the long-nose model, most agree that further improvements in tin worm avoidance had taken place. It's fair to say that, generally, unless a T4 has been neglected for a number of years, or involved in an accident and shoddily repaired, serious rust is not likely to be a problem. Also, from '96 onwards, the front wings were bolted on, making accident damage in that vicinity easier to repair.

When the T4 was launched, VW made great play of the safety features built-in as standard. They proclaimed the merits of "a rigid 'safety cell' with crumple zones to absorb crash energy, and side impact protection." Additionally, components of the chassis and body were deformable and, of course, the steering column was collapsible. However, VW also shouted that the "precise" design of both chassis and suspension, aided "directional stability." Disc brakes were cited, as was the invariably optional extra of ABS and traction control – possibly things we take for granted today, but then by no means universal.

With usage, life expectancy and health and safety discussed, how about some basics; all Volkswagens sport air-cooled engines and are rear-wheel drive, right? Wrong on all counts: the T4 was the first Transporter to sport a front-mounted engine and front-wheel drive, as per the VW Golf, Polo, Passat etc, etc. It was also the second model of Transporter to carry a water-cooled engine, and the second to be offered with diesel options. It was the second to offer VW's synchro all-wheel drive system as an option, and the third to make the left foot redundant with one form or another of automatic transmission. To date it is unique in Transporter history in terms of having a new front end devised but the old design not becoming a thing of the past.

The Colorado, coach-built in Germany by Karmann, is a fine example of the spacious and comfortable Campers readily available on a T4 Chassis Cab.

Reimo and many others produced high-specification traditional Campers based on the SWB T4. The 2.5TDI engine ensures reasonable power and economy.

For harmonious living with a T4, we'd tentatively suggest that out of the multitude of engine options available over the production run, the best bet is the 2.5-litre, five-cylinder, direct injection, turbocharged and intercooled diesel: an engine that offers 102PS at 3500rpm. Assuming you can tolerate its thirst, the petrol engine 2.8 VR6 is worthy of consideration, or, better still, its successor for the 2001 model year, the 24-valve V6, which boasted a top speed of 120mph and a capability to cover 0-60mph in just 10.9 seconds. A downside for some concerning both the VR6 and V6, certainly as far as the UK market is concerned, is that it was only available linked to an auto box.

Finally, some might suggest that the above engines also offer the best deal, as their introductions date from the years 1996 onwards, and are linked to the more aesthetically pleasing long-nose T4. In response, we'd say there was little wrong with the more powerful earlier engine options, and some owners prefer the appearance of the short-nose models.

4 Relative values
– which model for you?

If you have read the preceding chapters, you are probably already aware of what we are going to say here. We are advocating being willing to pay that little bit extra to get your hands on a later model T4 endowed with the 2.5TDI engine. With power to keep up with the crowd where necessary, coupled to well-known diesel longevity, the 2.5TDI has to be a best buy, while the appearance of the long-nose models is more in keeping with contemporary styling.

Whatever the guise, our recommendation is to regard the 2.5TDI T4 as a best buy. This example is a Caravelle.

102PS 2.5-litre TDI badging.

For petrol power the VR6 is okay, if somewhat thirsty. Here's the beast in Caravelle form. Note that in the early days standard spec didn't extend to alloys.

Of the rest, a VR6 or V6 is an expensive luxury to run, and the older diesels offer pedestrian performance, which should be reflected in the asking price. However, one other consideration has to be taken into account: if it's a Camper, or even a weekender (Multivan) you are after, the reputation, quality and condition of the conversion will definitely have a bearing on the price.

A bespoke interior added to a T4 in recent years is always worthy of consideration, especially where one of the many reputable craftsman builders has been involved, but be suspicious if such a T4 appears cheap. Oh, and some like the luxury of a T4 motorhome, but they remain relatively costly.

What it says on the back of the VR6 tin!

Better than the VR6, the V6 was both more powerful and comparatively frugal.

Transporters
Various less powerful engines on offer, from a wide range of years, and tend to be high mileage. Average in good body condition, ●x3000 to ●x5000.

Caravelles
Later models with a 2.5TDI engine, with average mileage lower than Transporters. Only above-average appearance considered, ●x5000 to ●x7000.

Campers
All years, but only top condition considered. Recognised professional conversion ●x7000 to ●x15,000 and beyond (add ●x2000 min to motorhome prices); professional bespoke conversion ●x7000 to ●x13,000; homespun conversion ●x6000 to ●x12,000.

5 Before you view

– be well informed

To avoid a wasted journey, and the disappointment of finding that the car does not match your expectations, it will help if you're very clear about what questions you want to ask before you pick up the telephone. Some of these points might appear basic, but when you're excited about the prospect of buying your dream classic, it's amazing how some of the most obvious things slip the mind ... Also check the current values of the model you are looking for in classic car magazines which give both a price guide and auction results.

Where is the car?

Is it going to be worth travelling to the next county/state, or even across a border? A locally advertised car, although it may not sound very interesting, can add to your knowledge for very little effort, so make a visit – it might even be in better condition than expected.

Dealer or private sale

Establish early on if the car is being sold by its owner or by a trader. A private owner should have all the history, so don't be afraid to ask detailed questions. A dealer may have more limited knowledge of a car's history, but should have some documentation. A dealer may offer a warranty/guarantee (ask for a printed copy) and finance.

Cost of collection and delivery

A dealer may well be used to quoting for delivery by car transporter. A private owner may agree to meet you halfway, but only agree to this after you have seen the car at the vendor's address to validate the documents. Conversely, you could meet halfway and agree the sale but insist on meeting at the vendor's address for the handover.

View – when and where

It is always preferable to view at the vendor's home or business premises. In the case of a private sale, the car's documentation should tally with the vendor's name and address. Arrange to view only in daylight and avoid a wet day. Most cars look better in poor light or when wet.

Reason for sale

Do make it one of the first questions. Why is the car being sold and how long has it been with the current owner? How many previous owners?

Left-hand drive to right-hand drive/specials and convertibles

If a steering conversion has been done it may reduce the value, and it may well be that other aspects of the car still reflect the specification for a foreign market.

Condition (body/chassis/interior/mechanicals)

Ask for an honest appraisal of the car's condition. Ask specifically about some of the check items described in chapter 7.

All original specification
An original equipment car is invariably of higher value than a customised version.

Matching data/legal ownership
Do VIN/chassis, engine numbers and licence plate match the official registration document? Is the owner's name and address recorded in the official registration documents?

For those countries that require an annual test of roadworthiness, does the car have a document showing it complies (An MOT certificate in the UK, which can be verified on 0300 123 9000 / www.gov.uk/check-mot-status)?

If a smog/emissions certificate is mandatory, does the car have one?

If required, does the car carry a current road fund licence/licence plate tag?

Does the vendor own the car outright? Money might be owed to a finance company or bank: the car could even be stolen. Several organisations will supply the data on ownership, based on the car's licence plate number, for a fee. Such companies can often also tell you whether the car has been 'written-off' by an insurance company. In the UK these organisations can supply vehicle data:

DVLA – 0844 453 0118
HPI – 0113 222 2010
AA – 0800 056 8040
RAC – 0330 159 0364
Other countries will have similar organisations.

Unleaded fuel
If necessary, has the car been modified to run on unleaded fuel?

Insurance
Check with your existing insurer before setting out, your current policy might not cover you to drive the car if you do purchase it.

How you can pay
A cheque/check will take several days to clear and the seller may prefer to sell to a cash buyer. However, a banker's draft (a cheque issued by a bank) is as good as cash, but safer, so contact your own bank and become familiar with the formalities that are necessary to obtain one.

Buying at auction
If the intention is to buy at auction see chapter 10 for further advice.

Professional vehicle check (mechanical examination)
There are often marque/model specialists who will undertake professional examination of a vehicle on your behalf. Owners clubs will be able to put you in touch with such specialists.

Other organisations that will carry out a general professional check in the UK:

AA – 0800 056 8040 / www.theaa.com/vehicle-inspection (motoring organisation with vehicle inspectors)

RAC – 0330 159 0720 / www.rac.co.uk/buying-a-car/vehicle-inspections (motoring organisation with vehicle inspectors)

Other countries will have similar organisations.

This book
Reading glasses (if you need them for close work)
Magnet (not powerful, a fridge magnet is ideal)
Torch
Probe (a small screwdriver works very well)
Overalls
Mirror on a stick
Digital camera
A friend, preferably a knowledgeable enthusiast

Before you rush out of the door, gather together a few items that will help as you work your way around the car. This book is designed to be your guide at every step, so take it along and use the check boxes to help you assess each area of the car you're interested in. Don't be afraid to let the seller see you using it.

Take your reading glasses if you need them to read documents and make close up inspections.

A magnet will help you check if the car is full of filler, or has fibreglass panels. Use the magnet to sample bodywork areas all around the car, but be careful not to damage the paintwork. Expect to find a little filler here and there, but not whole panels. There's nothing wrong with fibreglass panels, but a purist might want the car to be as original as possible.

A torch with fresh batteries will be useful for peering into the wheelarches and under the car.

A small screwdriver can be used – with care – as a probe, particularly in the wheelarches and on the underside. With this you should be able to check an area of severe corrosion, but be careful – if it's really bad the screwdriver might go right through the metal!

Be prepared to get dirty. Take along a pair of overalls, if you have them. Fixing a mirror at an angle on the end of a stick may seem odd, but you'll probably need it to check the condition of the underside of the car. It will also help you to peer into some of the important crevices. You can also use it, together with the torch, along the underside of the sills and on the floor.

If you have the use of a digital camera, take it along so that later you can study some areas of the car more closely. Take a picture of any part of the car that causes you concern, and seek a friend's opinion.

Ideally, have a friend or knowledgeable enthusiast accompany you: a second opinion is always valuable.

7 Fifteen minute evaluation
– walk away or stay?

This is our quick but significant guide. We've already said that nobody needs to buy a rusty or neglected T4. If that's what you find on arrival at a viewing, walk away immediately.

Exterior

A T4 should exhibit nothing more than slight traces of surface rust and, preferably, will be completely free of the dreaded tin-worm. With the arrival of the long-nose model for the '96 model year still greater attention was paid to rust prevention. You shouldn't be finding much, if any, but, as a rust-seeking sleuth, where are you most likely to track it down?

The usual candidates for the occurrence of rust are the edges of the wheelarches (an inevitable possibility considering winter driving conditions and liberal doses of salt, plus cheaply repaired roads covered with those dreaded loose chippings), the lower sills (similar story), the area adjoining the lowest reaches of the windscreen and the base of the sliding door (a seemingly weak point), both inside and out. Anything within these categories will undoubtedly cost money to repair and you should probably walk away.

Take care, though, as visible rust isn't your only enemy. Equally destructive is rust that lies concealed beneath paint, its first appearance coming in the form of bubbles. Eventually they burst, but by such time are pretty obvious to see. Keep your eyes focused and walk away if you find anything of this nature.

What are this T4's assets? It's a later model, so has more rust protection; it's original, to use as is, or as a canvas, and a tailgate rather than doors provides added value.

A great deal of well-engineered work has been done here. This vehicle started life with a short nose ... always ask and check.

Just what you wanted, but have you considered what the graphics may hide, and how they may affect potential resale values – a rule that applies to all customised T4s?

Where owners have caused damage with dings and bashes to panels and no attempt has been made to repair and protect exposed metal (again, wheelarches appear prone to knocks and scrapes, while along the sides of vehicles scratches and gouging, often caused by travelling on narrow roads, are prevalent), you don't need to waste your time further.

However, supposing you are determined to buy a Delivery Van with the intention of turning it into a Camper. The chances are that there could be one or several distortions to the side panels. These are caused by heavy items being rather casually loaded into the Bus. Providing the paint surface isn't cracked or broken, and assuming it is your intention to respray your purchase anyway, you should carry out a more detailed analysis of the damage as part of a serious evaluation. If distortion isn't your cup of tea it will be back to scouring the adverts.

A mismatch of colours between panels is often an indication of poor remedial work following damage, while flat paintwork sounds warning bells of longer term neglect (red vehicles are particularly prone to the effects of sunlight on infrequently waxed and polished paint). Bringing a T4 back to the way it left the Hanover factory isn't difficult, assuming you are prepared to use a little elbow grease and quantities of proprietary products such as T-Cut or Autoglym's Paint Renovator. Oh, and as a general rule, 'ordinary' paint is usually easier to bring back to a sparkle than either metallic or pearlescent panels. However, why should you slave away when there are better examples out and about? Also consider that if there are visible signs of neglect, it is highly likely that hidden gremlins could well apply to mechanical aspects of the vehicle.

Being a couple of world-wise fuddy-duddies, we would view a heavily modified T4 with suspicion, wary that tasks had been carried out in a slipshod manner. Graphics, for example, might be one owner's pleasure, while to others they do nothing to add value and could easily detract from the T4's worth. Similarly, a colour change isn't welcome to many buyers. On that 15-minute look, our advice would be to ask yourself whether you're sure, before you take your viewing further.

Finally, neither of us would touch a T4 Camper where there is evidence that the roof leaks. Again, there are plenty of good examples about, so why pick one with a visible problem and something that could well mask hidden horrors?

15 minutes of sheer joy, this T4 ticks all your boxes. Deal done! Whoops, it won't fit in the garage. The Winnebago Rialta has a length of 6299mm.

Not conversant with what's what? Long-nose T4s have headlamps that slope towards the centre of the vehicle. Note well the signs of visible neglect!

Interior

What are the key points about an interior? In our view they have to be (in alphabetical order): dashboard, door cards, fixtures and fittings, headlining, and upholstery, while with a Camper you need to add equipment to that list. Clock up negatives and – you've guessed it – time to walk away.

As far as the dash goes, it would be unusual, considering the vagaries of our climate, but you may come across a dashboard split by the effects of sunlight. You are more likely to encounter holes 'drilled' to house accessories, permanently disfiguring glue, irritating stickers that may prove impossible to remove without damage, and so on. You will be able to acquire a replacement, but think of the hassle …

Replacing a door card (or other trim for that matter) is relatively easy, and T4s aren't anywhere near as prone to the consequences of giant speakers being cut into panels as are earlier models. Find a T4 that has this kind of damage and we know what we would do.

Fixtures and fittings are slightly different. Here, we are looking at the working order of all the items supplied by Volkswagen as part of the original specification, plus all those items successive owners have added over the years. During a 15-minute evaluation there won't be time to make sure everything works, but at least broken switches and missing bits and pieces will be obvious. Be wary as you enter the next stage!

Modern-day headlinings are nowhere near as easy to clean as old-fashioned white vinyl, but they are less prone to rips and tears. Minor marks – such as greasy finger-marks, or where someone's head has touched the roof – can invariably be removed with hot water, a liberal application of soap, and patience! Gouge the headlining and the damage is permanent. Replacement headlinings can be acquired, but, again, is it worth it?

Search hard enough and you should find leatherette upholstery on a more workaday T4. However, most models feature cloth, a better proposition in warm weather. You might even come across a really posh T4 with leather upholstery. Leatherette is robust but unpalatable, and hardly conducive to all but workaday practices. Cloth is lovely, as it breathes, but sadly VW invariably offered light coloured options that are prone to dirt and stains; many hours are required to get them back to pristine condition (if you are lucky). Cloth is also much more vulnerable to things like a bunch of keys worn on a belt eating their way into the material, damaging it permanently. Cloth fades too, although as yet there is little evidence of material disintegrating thanks to the effects of the sun. Light coloured leathers (which do exist) look dirty as the years go by, while all leathers should be 'fed' at least once a year to keep them supple. Pick a T4 with as little wear and tear as possible. If the seats are 'shot,' it's odds-on that the rest of the vehicle won't be brilliant.

Finally, the Camper: everything above still applies, but you need to add the T4's camping equipment to the list. Items that don't work, the conversion company's carpeting, upholstery, insulation, and the generosity or sparsity of the cooking, washing and sleeping facilities; all have to be taken into account. Our advice for a 15-minute assessment in this area is, do you like the look of the camping arrangements? If the answer is yes, delve further in your serious evaluation. If it's no, exit stage left as quickly as possible!

Cloth upholstery wears and tears more than yucky special order vinyl. Plastic dash might possibly crack, and there is much to check in the back.

Mechanicals

Most mechanical components on a T4 are readily available, and the majority are reasonably priced, especially when purchased from independent VW specialists. An exception is the automatic gearbox, as both parts and repair can prove to be very expensive, likewise any part relevant to the four-wheel-drive syncro system. Under the bonnet the engine and components should be reasonably clean, with nothing obviously broken and everything you would expect to find in place. Viewing the engine and ancillaries under the bonnet is difficult due to the cramped nature of the engine compartment (see serious evaluation for a solution). It is possible to check that the brake fluid is topped up to the recommended level and there are no tell-tale drips of coolant emanating from the radiator. The battery is on the left-side-rear of the engine bay, but is difficult to access unless the vendor is willing to undo the catches and remove the cover. If the cover is missing, the battery may have been charged before your visit or someone has been careless.

A recurrent theme of the guide is your reason for purchasing a T4. This is particularly relevant to a quick evaluation and the vehicle's engine. Many sellers will advertise that their T4 is a diesel or petrol model, but most won't declare a specific engine. If your intention is to use the vehicle as you would a modern-day Transporter, you would probably be wise to avoid the slower, more pedestrian offerings and particularly those of the earlier years. If you imagine yourself tootling about as you might with an earlier air-cooled Transporter, such engines are more likely to be acceptable. Here we will outline the options which might suit your purpose and indicate any offerings which it is probably best to avoid.

At launch, the UK market Transporter (Delivery Vans, basic vans with windows and chassis cabs) was offered with two petrol engines and two diesels. They were:

They are not all as clean as this, and they're definitely not the easiest to inspect, but it's worth the effort having memorised our words of wisdom in this section.

a petrol four-cylinder 1.8-litre 67PS, a petrol four-cylinder 2.0-litre 84PS (also available with catalytic converter), a diesel four-cylinder 1.9-litre 61PS, and a diesel five-cylinder 2.4-litre 78PS. The people-carrying Caravelles were offered with an additional petrol engine, the fuel-injected five-cylinder 2.5-litre 110PS. The 61PS diesel engine was not a Caravelle option. We would not put any of these engines towards the top of our recommended list, and anyone contemplating the 61PS diesel should demonstrate patience. Talking to owners, we have concluded that most problems relate to the 2.4-litre diesel engines.

By 1994 the petrol 1.8-litre 67PS was no longer available, while the petrol five-cylinder 110PS engine had become an option for Transporter purchasers. The petrol 2.5-litre and diesel 2.4-litre engines were both available in four-speed automatic guise as well as manual mode. During the same year a four-cylinder 1.9-litre 'Umwelt' turbo diesel developing 68PS was added and made available to Caravelle users. 'Umwelt' (meaning 'environment') was a marketing theme for VW around this time, but the concept evaporated without a trace within a remarkably short period.

1996 saw the introduction of a restyled T4 with a longer front end. This long-nose version was developed to accommodate the new VR6 petrol engine, but all Caravelle options benefited from the re-styled front end. Transporters retained the short-nose. The 2.8-litre 140PS six-cylinder VR6 petrol engine (only available as an automatic in the UK) was accompanied by the 2.5-litre five-cylinder 110PS petrol engine. The 2.4-litre five-cylinder 78PS diesel, now branded as the SD, was accompanied by a new diesel engine which heads our recommended list. This is the five-cylinder 2.5-litre 102PS TDI (direct injection, turbocharged and intercooled); the first 'modern' VW diesel engine with a reputation for both power and economy.

Transporter engine options were now: petrol 2.0-litre four-cylinder 84PS, petrol 2.5-litre five-cylinder 110 PS, diesel four-cylinder 1.9-litre TD 68PS, diesel five-cylinder 2.4-litre SD 78PS, and the new five-cylinder 2.5-litre 102PS TDI.

In 2000 further changes occurred; the VR6 was replaced by the V6. This petrol engine not only had more power than its predecessor, but crucially offered greater economy. The 2.8-litre 24-valve V6 offered 204PS, a maximum speed of 120mph, 0-60mph in 10.9 seconds, and overall fuel economy of 34mpg. Unlike its predecessor, the V6 was not de-tuned and is our recommendation for anyone keen to a) opt for petrol, and b) arrive early. Note, however, that in the UK, the V6 was only available as an automatic.

Following the success of the diesel 102PS TDI, an efficient but less powerful version was added in 1999. This was the five-cylinder 2.5-litre 88PS TDI, which offered a top speed of 96mph and overall fuel economy of 35.7mpg (compared to 98mph and 36.6 mpg for the 102PS version), and is another of our recommended engines. A third TDI engine of the same vintage, which offered a sparkling 150PS, was only available in Germany and selected European mainland markets.

With the engine desirability confirmed, check the service history to establish when the toothed camshaft drivebelt (on all models) and the fuel pump drivebelt (on the five-cylinder models) were last changed. Both should be changed at 60,000 miles – especially if the belts show signs of deterioration – and certainly no later than 80,000 miles, or every four years. A lack of service history is not necessarily a reason to walk away from a T4 in good condition, but be cautious.

Check the exhaust system, especially on petrol-powered models, as corrosion from within the exhaust is more likely. A little oil under the engine is acceptable, but it is advisable to examine the underside of the area for oil and fluid leaks. Excessive oil under the engine could indicate a defective cylinder head gasket or crankshaft oil seal. You may be hampered by the presence of the factory-fitted engine under-tray. Check the oil level and the condition of the oil. Ask if additional oil is needed between services. Ask the vendor to start the engine to check for excessive exhaust smoke. Smoke may be visible on start-up, but even diesel models should tick over smoothly with no visible fumes (increasingly stringent MOT emission rules imply visible smoke could be an issue with diesels). If the engine shakes in its mountings every now and then when ticking over, it may indicate problems with the dual-mass flywheel. This will settle down when the engine speed is increased but any other knocks or rattles from the engine may indicate a more expensive future problem. A rattle from a hydraulic tappet will indicate replacement shortly.

If alloy wheels are fitted, do a visual inspection of the disc brakes – front and rear – on all models produced after May 1996. Self-adjusting drum brakes were fitted to the rear previously.

There is a four-wheel drive T4 syncro version available that uses the five-cylinder engines only. The syncro has permanent 4WD and the transmission to the rear axle is through a viscous coupling that provides torque to the rear axle. Spare transmission parts for these models are expensive.

Only buy a T4 from an individual who can prove that they are the person named in the vehicle's registration document (V5C in the UK) and, preferably, at the address shown in the document. Also check that the VIN or chassis number/frame and engine numbers of the car/motorcycle match the numbers in the registration document.

Check the wheelarches (especially front right), sills, and door bottoms for rust. Check panels for scratches and parking scrapes. Check external mirrors for scrapes and functionality. Check sliding door for slippage. Check wheels for rust and alloys for kerbing.

Check bonnet for rusty stone chips and rust below windscreen. Check for rust creeping out from under rubber seals. Check windscreen for chips/cracks. Check headlamps, etc, for misting, cracks, or an opaque appearance. Check plastic grille for cracks, and the bumper for scrapes.

Check tailgate for rust at base. Look at all the paint/bumper/general rust points on the previous page and apply here. Don't forget to check the light clusters. Check the roof panel for rust blemishes. For Campers, check elevating roof functionality/leaks.

Confirm the engine is correct for the model viewed. Check the condition of hoses, radiator, intercooler – if fitted – and all ancillaries. Be wary of non-standard wiring, especially if it appears to bypass components. Look for oil leaks from head gasket.

Check the headlining, cloth upholstery (tears, stains), carpets/matting (any trace of dampness), trim panels and dash (damage/holes). Check instrument panel for functionality, heater, window mechanism (electric or manual). If a Camper, check all appliances work and units are free from damage.

9 Serious evaluation
– 60 minutes for years of enjoyment

If you have successfully completed the 15-minute evaluation in chapter 7, and want to see more, now is the time for a full and thorough check over the vehicle. Score each section using the boxes as follows: 4 = excellent; 3 = good; 2 = average; 1 = poor. The totting-up procedure is detailed at the end of the chapter. Be realistic in your marking!

Exterior
Paint

As Concours judges of many years standing, we consider the best way to evaluate most aspects of a vehicle – but particularly paint – is to work methodically over the whole body, invariably starting with the roof panel. Detailed scrutiny will locate any blemishes, while the touch of a hand unfettered by rings, or anything else likely to scratch, will confirm the depth of protective polish.

The roof of a T4, thanks to its relative inaccessibility, is likely to be the panel that is washed less often, polished infrequently, and not subject to the instant removal of items like bird-dirt or tree sap. However, its distance from the road also ensures it is less vulnerable to the wear and tear of daily driving. Any untreated stone chips are likely to be found towards the front of the panel, above the windscreen. Occasionally someone might have climbed about on the roof panel causing damage, but you should be able to spot that with an initial glance. As the roof is a long way from the ground, ask to borrow the seller's steps, or bring a pair with you in the boot of your vehicle.

The most vulnerable panels, as far as stone chips are concerned, are the bonnet and anything else located at the front of the vehicle. You should confirm that all chips have been dealt with using one of Volkswagen's own touch-up kits or an appropriate

T4s are susceptible to front end/bonnet stone chips. Some fastidious owners add a bonnet bib which, if left on permanently, can be a water trap.

Check that any bonnet chips have been attended to. Consider the cost of a required bonnet respray ... negotiate on the price of the vehicle!

Rusty sills shouldn't be entertained. Look elsewhere. This is non-negotiable if you want to protect your bank balance.

Wheelarch rust disfigures the most attractive of T4s, and is expensive to eradicate. The arch closest to the ventilation grille is most vulnerable.

Beware: to make this good again, you are looking at cutting out the rust. With numerous T4s available, you don't need to buy one like this.

substitute. Untreated chips will eventually result in rust spots. Clumsy touch-up work will annoy you, but won't add further damage to what could soon be your T4. Occasionally, the front edge of a bonnet might display corrosion or bubbling. If this is apparent, it is unlikely that the rest of the vehicle will be in a suitable condition to contemplate purchase.

When checking side panels, always run your hands round the wheelarches. Salt and loose chippings will inevitably take their toll. Some owners may apply a dose of protective wax, such as Waxoyl, while the really fastidious will treat the arches as simply another area to polish to perfection. Others may go to the lengths of re-spraying the arch edges, or for the perfect finish have a professional do it for them. Be suspicious if there is caked-on dirt and mud in this area, which may have led to damage to the bodywork through neglect.

Side panels are prone to scratches where someone has driven too close to a hedge, or even a stone wall, on a narrow road. People push alongside vehicles in car parks, scratch the paint in the vicinity of the handle as they open the T4's doors, are careless and let an open door touch a wall or another vehicle, while the malicious might think it amusing to run a key along a pristine panel. Minor scratches will polish out, but deeper scrapes will always show. Having a door edge professionally tidied, or particularly a key scrape removed, will be relatively expensive as it is likely that a whole panel will be repainted. You should not consider a T4 where bare metal has been exposed and allowed to rust.

Always run your hands under the bottom of each door – another case of 'out of sight, out of mind' for some owners. Rust here is certainly a negative, but you might possibly think that carrying out remedial work here will be less costly, as it can be a DIY job as the results will not be readily visible.

Keep an eye open for rust creeping out from a rubber seal. T4s are not known for this often-worse-than-it-looks problem, but better safe than sorry.

Rust can form in the rear corner of the cab door window apertures on a neglected van. Our advice: visible neglect is often the tip of the iceberg. Walk away!

What about bulges on a Delivery Van's panels – the kind created by loads banging into the panels? If the paint hasn't been breached, there is little risk of rust. However, such deformities are ugly and will take both time and patience to remove. Some people relish the task, while a professional will simply see a steady trickle of larger denomination notes.

To summarise, what you would have looked at during your 15-minute evaluation is repeated here in more detail, and we add a few extra considerations. Faded paint can be rectified with a bit of work; a professional company will do it for you, but your wallet will be lighter as a result. Fading implies neglect! A panel, or panels, that vary in colour from the rest might mean accident damage (which you would need to talk about) or simply a cheap makeover. Check where paint meets rubber, and if you can see a 'line' where original paint meets new paint, your suspicions are confirmed – a case of a quick masking and splash of paint.

Finally, on the subject of panels and paint, you won't be carrying out a serious evaluation if you come across a T4 with rust in any of the following areas: immediately below the windscreen, those all-important wheelarches, the sills, and the bottoms of the doors. Add the area around the filler cap just to be sure. To be doubly sure, turn your attention to the chassis, such as it is, the floorpan and the inner wings. Rust might also have found its way to the crossmember in the vicinity of the rear springs. It's highly likely that if you find rust in any of these locations you will already have come across problems elsewhere.

What is this? Yes, check the roof, as the longitudinal strips over it may well conceal rust.

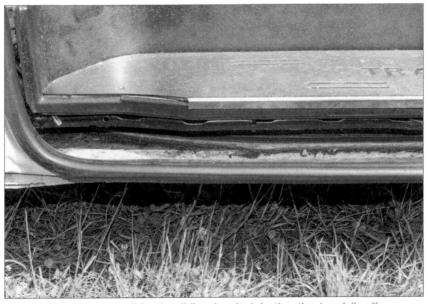

Okay, if the top rail for the sliding door is defective, the door falls off. This is the bottom and should be much better.

T4s are not prone to problems in this area. However, if anything is going to go adrift, it is most likely to be the vehicle's sliding door. If the top rail is worn the normal smooth and easy opening and closing action may not be apparent, and in extreme circumstances the door can simply drop out. Lifting the door up and down will confirm whether there is play. Also, if it doesn't sit flush when closed, beware, although adjustments can be made to ensure it fits correctly.

Inside affecting outside! Check under the rubber matting/carpets in the cab for rust such as this.

Exterior trim and seals ⊠ ⊠ ⊠ ⊠

Examine the seals on your potential purchase to ensure all are watertight. There should be at least an inkling of water ingress if all is not good. Most vulnerable to failure, partial or otherwise, is the area around the bottom of the tailgate. For the future, a light dusting with talc every now and then is alleged to keep the rubber supple, while if you need to replace a seal, quality ones are readily available from a number of suppliers at realistic prices.

Concerning trim, we often think that you can tell a lot about a Bus and its keeper by the state of these accessories. Without too obviously harping on about paint once more, are the colour-coded bumpers the subject of one or more parking scrapes? In terms of damage that's likely to cause deterioration in the condition of the vehicle, there isn't any. However, aesthetically, scrapes revealing black plastic are annoying. Having a bumper resprayed doesn't cost a fortune, but most professionals will want to do the whole bumper. The same goes for colour-coded wing mirrors. A friend with a T4 who used to have colour-coded wing mirrors eventually succumbed and replaced them with simple black plastic ones. He

If seals aren't up to scratch, water will sneak in and lay tin-worm eggs.
Door handles can harbour rust in their vicinity – worth checking.

lives down a narrow well-used road. He might be careful, clearly other drivers are not. Bumper scrapes are likely to be the fault of the driver; mirror damage might well be the responsibility of others.

This leads us nicely in to bumpers that haven't been colour-coded. Leave them as they are, with nothing more than a wash every now and then, and they will fade. What was black will become grey, bleached by the elements. Proprietary cleaners – one named 'Back to Black' springs to mind – keep bumpers looking good, and, in all but the worst instances of bleaching, do what they say on the tin. Again, though, would you trust a man who drives a T4 with badly bleached bumpers?

The rubber seals around door openings can hide rust and are often neglected.

If electric, does the mirror work? Is the 'frame' cracked or damaged?

Colour-coded mirror housings on posh T4s. If the paint's scraped, most people should be able to rectify this, but professional labour is expensive.

Essentially, there isn't a great deal of trim on a T4, and what there is tends to be held firmly in place. There was a penchant for stealing the VW roundel from the front grille, while it is just possible that someone may decide to enhance the badging on the rear of the vehicle to imply a status beyond what was attributed by VW. Be honest, though: would you fall for the trick of a Caravelle with vinyl seats? It's best to suggest you check that the grille area on your T4 isn't damaged or broken. Even the long-nose front area is made out of plastic, and there may be cracks or breaks in the material.

Wipers
We haven't heard of issues with wiper motors or anything else that could impede a journey on a wet day. However, if you are contemplating presenting the T4 for MOT yourself, you should remember that if the washers don't issue enough liquid to clear the screen the vehicle will fail, just as it will if the wipers are insecure, or if the blades are in a condition where they don't clear the windscreen sufficiently well for the driver to see the road ahead.

Glass
All T4s are subject to an annual MOT. Be careful when it comes to checking the vehicle's windscreen. The rules state a maximum of 10mm damage in the field of the driver's vision (that's in front of the steering wheel to a tune of 290mm) and 40mm anywhere else that the windscreen wipers sweep. A chipped screen is easily replaced, and an aftermarket version won't cost mega bucks. A damaged screen wouldn't deter a purchase if all else was well, but you might use the 'd' word; yes, discount!

Lights

Broken or cracked covers/lenses will require replacement, whether they are at the back or front of the vehicle. Similarly, if the reflectors are tarnished, or the headlamp 'cover' is scratched, misted, or opaque, you are looking at purchasing replacements. A multiplicity of options exists, ranging from OE (original equipment) spec examples, cheaper aftermarket copies, the option to upgrade to LEDs and, of course, custom products. Beware, though: replacing a headlamp or rear light cluster is not a quick single-note job, and if the light clusters all need replacing, how can the rest of the vehicle be worthy of serious consideration?

Cracked or broken lens covers will require replacement.

Headlight clusters: if the reflector is tarnished, or the 'cover' scratched, misted or opaque, you need to replace immediately.

Chrome accents, daytime running lights and integral indicators; a custom unit possibly worth considering. Effective, certainly, stylish, too ... but not cheap.

Wheels and tyres

Most T4s were supplied with steel wheels, while Volkswagen offered a series of alloys as extra cost accessories. Some steel wheels were essentially bereft of a wheel trim, other than a cap at the centre. Others, usually models with a higher spec, would benefit from full-size plastic trims, finished in silver and offered in a variety of designs over the years. All will be aware that steel rims invariably exhibit signs of rust as the years go by, whether the wheel is painted silver (centre cap) or black (full trim). Your actions are determined by your love of aesthetics. What rust there is will do no harm to the vehicle. You keep painting your wheels, or replace the plastic trims if you scuff them – simple as that. Rusty wheels should not deter a purchase.

The wheel might be unsightly, but it isn't structurally dangerous. Hours can be spent with a wire brush and a spray can, but rust will reappear.

Don't want alloys; don't like rusty wheels? Here's the answer: official VW or aftermarket wheel trims.

This very attractive set of official VW alloys cost the owner £500 in 1999 ... kerbed or corroded alloys cost a lot to make good.

Many aftermarket alloys are suitable for the T4. This is a Dare 20in LG2 wheel. Check any fitted aftermarket alloys are suitable for the vehicle.

Kerbed alloys are unsightly but usually not dangerous. Repair/refurbishment of a set of four alloys will cost several hundred pounds on average (and also possibly involve new tyres). Alloys can also suffer from corrosion (characterised by flaking, lifting paint), something that is an aesthetic consideration rather than a safety one. Beware – alloys that are distorted or cracked could result in MOT failure.

For those who want to be rid of their steel wheels, there are many alloy aftermarket options available at a wide variety of prices.

Our advice regarding tyres is straightforward, and something only a new driver might not be aware of. If tread is low, or worn unevenly, ask for a discount; similarly, if budget tyres have been fitted, be suspicious of the brand and think discount. Check the safety rating of the tyres. If there is obvious damage to a tyre, ask why it is still on the vehicle, and don't forget to have a good look at the spare. One owner surprised us by saying that the spare was an alloy; five alloys, unusual!

Interior
How fussy should you be about a T4's interior, especially if your one aim in life is to rip out everything and create a Camper specific to your whims and needs? Only you can decide. All we can tell you is what to look for as standard.

Seats
[4] [3] [2] [1]

Unpleasant leatherette might be about on an older workhorse Transporter. This is easier to clean than cloth, and more durable than light-coloured fabric, plus you can always buy a set of seat covers. Leave it on view and expect to be stuck to the seats during the summer.

Cloth seat covers can easily become stained during use. Most marks can be cleaned away, but it's not a ten-minute job. Spot cleaning isn't really an option, as the area where one mark is removed will show up as cleaner than its surroundings. There are plenty of upholstery cleaners on the market, but sometimes a sponge, a bar of soap and hot water works just as well (if not better). Rips and tears are impossible to make good. New covers are available in a variety of OE patterns, but they are pricey.

Very posh T4s could well have leather upholstery. VW's leather is good, as might be expected, but it should be conditioned at least once a year to avoid it gradually becoming brittle and prone to cracking. Light colours are more difficult than black as, like a pair of light-coloured leather shoes, they eventually start to look grubby.

Watch out for faulty mechanisms, damaged armrests (if the T4 is sufficiently deluxe to have them), torn vinyl seat backs, and so on.

Virtually all T4s came with cloth upholstery. A number of designs were light-coloured, highlighting dirt which can be cleaned. Rips, burn holes, etc, can't.

If evaluating a Camper or Caravelle, remember there are more seats and fabric than what's on view in the cab. Beware also of covers that disguise or hide problems.

Some owners install leather-trimmed seats. Make sure that the skin has been fed at least once a year, to prevent cracking and general wear.

Carpets and mats

   □

With a workhorse model of any age, rubber is likely to abound. Durable and easy to spruce up when 'mucky,' wear and tear might have resulted in the odd hole where feet are frequently placed. An upgrade to carpet is always an option (see right). Carpeted T4s tend to be vehicles such as the luxury Caravelle. As it is highly unlikely that there will be any leaks, wet and smelly carpet is not on the agenda. Light colours are obviously more difficult to maintain. A wealth of carpets either mimicking OE specifications, or simply customised to your taste, are available and prices aren't extortionate.

Really upmarket models have carpet; most owners put carpet mats over moulded rubber. Lift for a damp check and generally inspect for dirt, wear and tear.

Evaluating a Camper, make sure to check the camping area floor covering.
Here is a good quality, dog-proof and countryside muck-proof rug
protecting what's underneath.

Headlining

The T4's headlining varies between models, but all are essentially rigid or moulded
in their nature, while looking as though they are made out of cloth. Marks are not
that easy to remove; think warm water, soap and a sponge again, and hope that
you can get away with feathering your way out of cleaning much more than the
area in the vicinity of the problem. More substantial damage, the odd gouge for
example, and you are stuck. A trawl on the net suggests the likes of eBay might
be an answer, and allegedly there are aftermarket kits available, too, though not
many.

Interior trim panels

The higher the spec of the T4 the more concealing and tasteful interior trim you are
likely to find. Bare metal is banished below stairs. In theory at least, whatever the
level of trim, it is likely to be of a robust plastic construction. It might be dirty, but is
fairly easy to clean. Do not use anything likely to leave a white residue when dealing
with plastic. Dashboard enhancers – preferably of a matt finish variety – help to
return the panel to good as new (almost).

Door locks and handles

The handles on wind-up windows can be broken, the winding mechanism suspect.
Replacements are readily available. If you are contemplating a high-spec model
with electric windows, check that all are operational and don't groan or creak. Apart
from the inconvenience of driving home on a wet winter's day with a window down

T4 door cards are made out of robust moulded plastic. They clean easily, but can be damaged by owners cutting holes!

Don't like plastic. This owner has 'flocked' the door cards … and it disguises damage, too, if necessary.

Door handles are generally robust. If the T4 you are evaluating has central locking, make sure it works efficiently.

A reasonable number of T4s have electric cab windows. Check they don't groan or creak when being lowered and lifted.

From windows to the instrument panel, don't forget to test the functionality of Camper electrics when evaluating.

because the mechanism has failed, the labour charges to rectify the fault is likely to bring a tear to your eye.

Similarly, check the central locking functionality as the labour is costly to fix the bits to make a temperamental unit good. Remember, the work involved, which includes taking off the door trim panel and, so we understand, lifting the glass out of the way. Labour doesn't come cheap.

You are already likely to have walked away from an interior which has been damaged by inappropriate accessories, holes for extraneous speakers etc. No rose-tinted specs please!

Dashboard and instrumentation

Let's look at some of the gadgetry operated from the instrument panel first. Inevitably, the more there is, the more that can go wrong. A sensible potential buyer will insist on operating every control to ensure full working order. Check the gauges too, as rumours abound of costly to replace faults. Try out the air-conditioning (yes, some models were so blessed), see if the six-CD interchanger will play your favourite tunes, and – more importantly – check out whether the indicators still self cancel and turn up the blower to make certain it doesn't screech.

Damage to the dashboard in terms of holes, marks, and the application of puerile stickers won't be that easy to disguise or repair. You might consider flocking the dash or – of course – fitting a replacement, but that is a fiddly exercise.

Some owners replace VW's steering wheel with one of their choice. However, standard units are very car-like in operation, and quite attractive.

Spend a little time making sure every knob, switch and stalk works as VW intended. Note the easy, pleasing-to-the-eye layout.

Apart from trimming the dashboard in leather, the owner of this T4 has changed the steering wheel. Work of this quality may increase the asking price.

You will spend a lot of time in the cab. The flocked dashboard and its leather and carpeted surroundings have to be to your liking.

The fuse and relay board is located under the right-hand side of the fascia, and is accessed after removing a small stowage box.

Secondhand units are widely advertised, so making the exchange isn't impossible. Again, the suspicion is that if the dashboard has been butchered, other things will be wrong too. With so many good T4s available, we could be tempted to look elsewhere rather than use our negotiating skills on this occasion.

Camper Vans

First, a quick reminder – Volkswagen did not make its own Camper until the advent of the T5. In Germany it worked closely with Westfalia, but RHD models for the British market were not part of the plan. Instead, VW licensed a number of manufacturers that offered conversions that could always be regarded as top notch. However, for many the fun of owning a VW Camper is in the creation of something bespoke to their needs, with large sums of money being spent to achieve their desired finish. In many cases these one-off

Auto-Sleepers Trooper – most T4 Campers come with a high specification. Key with this solid elevating roof model is that it doesn't leak.

Top-of-the-range Reimo Miami: roof check, tick; functionality of appliances check, tick; damage to units/work surfaces check, tick; auxiliary heating safe check, tick.

Holdsworth Vision XL: ah, the fixed high roof. Not for the average garage or city centre car park, but more spacious for you.

Auto-Sleepers Clubman GL: here, you are looking at glass-fibre monocoque coachwork, with home-from-home interior comforts and plenty of room. Interior materials haven't really aged.

The Westfalia California Exclusive: a big name in VW circles, and high spec ... but you are looking at a LHD Camper, which deters some.

interiors are just as good, if not better, than a standard conversion. Naturally, you would walk away from a Camper that appears amateurish in its build, odd in its composition, or at variance with your ideas of taste.

The key points to consider when evaluating a Camper with a view to purchase are very similar to probing the interior of any T4. Does the equipment work? Is anything damaged? Are things so dirty that a spruce up is going to be a major exercise? Do doors in the units drop? Does a work-surface exhibit the effects of heat? Does any form of auxiliary heating work, and is it safe? As far as we are concerned, possibly the most important issue is whether an elevating roof is completely weatherproof, and whether anything has been done with a homespun conversion to make the T4 potentially un-roadworthy or the cause of future issues.

Under the bonnet

It is sensible these days to take heed of the expression 'buyer beware,' and, with that in mind, the vendor shouldn't be offended if you ask about the T4's maintenance history and ask to have a look at the service records. While it would be unusual, it is not impossible that the vehicle has been looked after by a main Volkswagen dealer throughout its life and that a fully stamped service booklet exists. Even several years of main dealer servicing records would be advantageous. Nevertheless, the more likely scenario will be that the vehicle has been entrusted to an independent Volkswagen specialist (commendable), or a local garage or MOT centre (definitely acceptable) that has looked after family vehicles for many years, irrespective of the make of vehicle presented to them. In the latter case there may not be a full paper chase of bills, especially in the case of the local mechanic working on the vehicle in his spare time. Any paperwork is always better than nothing!

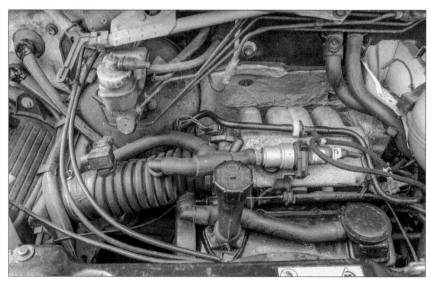

The relatively uncluttered appearance of this 2.0-litre petrol engine
is due to the lack of an intercooler.

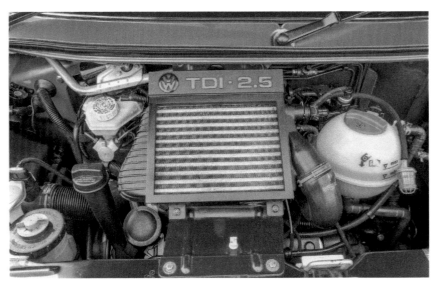

Engine accessibility is tight, especially when an intercooler is fitted. However, oil filler and other reservoirs are easily accessible on the 2.5TDI.

As with other aspects of your viewing, it is not a good idea to turn up on a wet day or within an hour of sunset. Seeing what you want to in the engine compartment of a T4 is difficult at the best of times, but next to impossible when natural light is poor. It is advisable to have a good torch to hand even on the sunniest of days.

Many of the operations and checks described in this section are likely to be more accessible with the radiator in the service position, vendor permitting. The seller may think this is going too far, so it is up to you if you decide to walk away at this point, especially if you think he or she is covering up something. Viewing the engine and components in the service position involves removing the radiator grille and the two bolts holding the upper radiator crossmember, before tilting the radiator forward and down. The hoses can stay connected during this operation. This is possible on all engine and body variants.

When looking under the bonnet of a T4, it is reasonable to expect to find a reasonably clean engine and ancillary components, except on a concours vehicle, where it should be approaching spotless. A dirty and untidy engine compartment would indicate to us that essential maintenance on the Bus has been neglected. On the other hand, a clean and tidy engine bay and a pile of service history documents would serve to give a potential buyer more confidence. The only caveat would be, beware an overly clean engine bay spruced up to make the vehicle appear more attractive to the potential buyer. Obviously, this will be up to you to decide, but we suggest that you would be unwise to proceed if the rest of the vehicle isn't up to the standard of the engine compartment. Many T4 owners have carried out modifications, so you may find a lot of non-standard components, such as an array of brightly-coloured silicon hoses, or an aftermarket air cleaner such as K&N. You may find that the engine has been modified in some way to achieve more power;

The airflow meter is an important component in the engine management system. It lurks in a hose adjacent to the windscreen washer filler.

the 2.5-litre models have an electronic control unit (ECU) that can have the internal chip replaced (known as mapping) to alter the power output parameters from those with which it left the factory. This is not always a good idea, as it is possible that such a modification will cause more diesel smoke. Many owners have fitted intercoolers to their 1.9-litre TD engines to give a boost to the otherwise somewhat leisurely power output. The power output of the 1.9TD engine should not put off a prospective purchaser; many owners have graduated from an earlier air-cooled model and are satisfied with the leisurely chilled-out lifestyle, and they may be over the moon that they can actually maintain 70mph when cruising on a motorway. One thing to be aware of with the 1.9-litre unit is a wobbly front pulley. The 1.9TD engine was inherited from the Mk3 Golf, and the problem occurs due to the keyway that locates the pulley becoming worn. This is often due to an incompetent mechanic, unfamiliar with this engine, removing the pulley by undoing the central bolt, rather than removing the four Allen bolts holding the outer pulley to the pulley hub. A loose pulley eventually fails when the keyway breaks, with disastrous consequences for the timing of the valve gear, the result of which is valves hitting the pistons. It is also possible, especially with the 1.9-litre units, that a TDI engine from another vehicle in the Volkswagen range has been fitted, along with all the components to make it operate properly. These 1.9- and 2.0-litre TDI engines (the latter was never an option as standard with a T4) are available with a huge range of higher power outputs than those originally fitted.

Using a torch, check under the engine for oil, water, or other fluid leaks. Also using the torch, have a good look around the engine bay for leaks of any sort. Space and access can be difficult, as there is very limited room, especially when an intercooler is fitted and appears to fill around a third of the area above the engine. A common fault is diesel fuel leaking from the rubber injector bleed-off pipes; this is usually detected by a strong smell of diesel and fuel dripping off the sump. An oil leak or oil and water contamination could indicate a head gasket failure, and this is an especially well known issue with 2.4-litre diesel units. There are a few tell-tale signs to look for, one of which is brown water stains down the side of the water top-up bottle, where the bottle has compressed due to increased pressure, causing the safety valve in the cap of the water bottle to blow the fluid out. The water bottle could also be contaminated internally, with rust particles and sludge from the engine block. Likewise, accessibility to view the underside of the engine and transmission is hampered by the engine compartment under tray. If, on closer

Check washer bottle and filler cap for damage and fit.

Ask if the 2.5TDI engine has been remapped for extra performance.

The intercooler obstructs much of the view on this 1.9TDI engine.

Water stains on the coolant expansion tank could indicate a head gasket fault. Examine the hoses and check that the expansion tank is sludge-free.

The oil filler cap is conveniently positioned at the front of the engine bay. Check for sludge in the cap and filler neck.

inspection, you can see oil on the under-body behind the engine it may be a cause for concern. Remove the oil filler cap and check for white frothy gunge. This may also indicate water contamination from a faulty head gasket, or maybe just condensation from a vehicle used for short journeys only. The 2.4-litre engines are also known for having problems with the cylinder head cracking between the valve seats. A cracked cylinder head can also be an issue with the 1.9-litre unit. However, it is unlikely that a T4 would be put up for sale with the cylinder head gasket leaking, as it would be virtually un-driveable, at least for any distance. There are plenty of good T4s available, so this could be a deal breaker; we would certainly walk away at this point. While a leaking head gasket is not a terminal fault, it will be expensive in labour time, especially if the cylinder head is found to be cracked when removed and examined on the bench. However, if you are a competent home mechanic, removal of the cylinder head and all related parts and operations are possible without removing the engine.

All other operations related to the engine block are carried out with the engine removed. It is possible to remove the 1.9-litre diesel engine without removing the gearbox. All other engine types are removed with the gearbox attached. However, engine removal isn't for the faint hearted, as the combined engine and gearbox assembly is extremely heavy.

Check that the clutch pedal operates smoothly. The bracket holding the pedal is known to bend and eventually break with metal fatigue. A repair plate is available to solve this problem. This is a well-known issue with the T4, as it gives a false impression of a faulty clutch, though early 2.4 diesel models have a different pedal box that is stronger. The clutch hydraulic master cylinder is mounted inside the cab, above the clutch pedal; consequently, a leaking cylinder will soak the carpet with hydraulic fluid. To gain access to the master cylinder, remove the small storage box to the right of the steering column. The 2.5-litre diesel models have a 02G transmission with the clutch slave cylinder within the bell housing. On these models, if the slave cylinder leaks it can contaminate the linings of the clutch friction plate. The 02B transmission used on the other models has an externally-mounted clutch slave cylinder.

We have already pointed out that it is a good idea to make sure all the switches and dials work correctly. This is especially true regarding the instrument panel, as it is fitted with a voltage regulator, which, when faulty, gives erratic readings of the fuel and temperature gauges.

While all engines in the range are perfectly usable and most owners are happy with their Bus whatever power unit is installed, there are two that we are selecting as the most desirable. Within the range of petrol units we feel the 24-valve, double overhead cam, 2.8-litre V6 engine is the pick of the

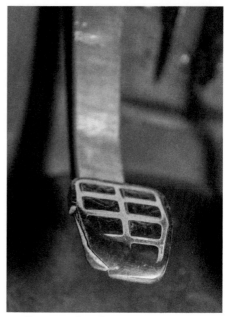

Feet can slip off worn pedal rubbers. A common fault: the bracket holding the pedal fails, causing crunching gears due to reduced movement.

Of the diesel models, we consider the 2.5TDI engine offering 102PS the pick of the bunch.

bunch, with 204PS at its disposal. The 12-valve, single overhead cam, 2.8-litre VR6 unit is less powerful, with 138PS available, and is reputed to be the thirstier of the two units.

Of the diesel units available, we would instinctively choose any of the inline five-cylinder 2.5-litre TDI engines that were introduced in 1995. These turbocharged direct injection units are available within our shores with an output of either 88PS or 102PS, while in Germany, a unit pushing out 150PS was available from 1998. Of course, it is possible that a few of these may have been personal imports to the UK, albeit with the controls on the left. This doesn't mean the other options are unworthy of consideration; indeed, most owners of a 1.9TD Bus are perfectly happy to cruise along at a leisurely pace. Just be aware of the dreaded front pulley wobble issue mentioned elsewhere in this section.

Wiring

Most of the wiring is hidden away under the dashboard, but the relays and fuse box can be accessed by removing the small storage box to the right of the steering column (see top image, p51). If everything looks okay here, it probably is. However, beware if you can see additional wiring not fitted at the time of manufacture, especially if it has been connected using connectors such as the blue clamp-together Scotchlok type.

Battery

Looking forward from the cab, the battery is fitted on the left rear of the engine bay and should be fitted with a cover that has a retaining catch and locating tabs to

The battery at the left rear of the engine compartment is usually covered by the housing for the air intake and pollen filter.

hold it in place. Lots of white corrosion around the battery terminals would indicate a battery that has been neglected during servicing. The battery cover also allows access to the pollen filter when it is removed. Battery technology has moved on in recent years, and should give a service life of three years plus. However, it is probably a false economy to buy a cheap battery; we would stick with reputable makes. Be wary if the sides of the battery look swollen, as this is a sign that it is past its best and could split – allowing corrosive acid to cause extensive damage to the surrounding bodywork.

Windscreen washer system

The windscreen washer jets should deliver a powerful stream of washer fluid to a point just above the centre of the windscreen and rear window. Most are adjustable using a pin, except on some models of T4 with nozzles that spray the fluid in a fan pattern across the screen.

Engine and transmission mountings

You are unlikely to find the following fault on a T4 put up for sale, but be aware that the three bolts on the right hand (offside) engine mounting of the 2.4-litre diesel engine have been known to shear, causing the engine mount to fail and dropping the engine on the right hand side. It may also be applicable to other engine types, but we haven't heard of any instances to verify it. If possible, attempt to rock the engine and transmission in its mountings; this may indicate that the rubber part of the engine mount is showing its age. If the metal part of the engine mount moves in relation to the vehicle body suspect problems with the aforementioned bolts.

Manifolds

When the engine is running, whistles or wheezing noises could be caused by a leaking cylinder head gasket or, equally importantly, a leaking inlet or exhaust manifold gasket. While the manifold gaskets are not expensive, the labour to replace them will be. Also, the noises could be due to a crack in the manifold, especially the exhaust manifold, the replacement of which could be expensive. We would not consider buying a T4 with an expensive fault, there are still plenty to choose from.

Fuel injection

All the diesel models are equipped with fuel-injection using a mechanical

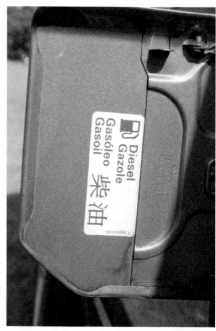

The sticker on the flap covering the fuel cap leaves no doubt what fuel must be used.

fuel pump. The 2.4-litre diesel engine is normally-aspirated, while the 1.9-litre TD and 2.5-litre TDI engines are boosted by a turbocharger. If the engine misfires, hesitates, or lacks power during acceleration, suspect at least one faulty injector. The turbocharger is mounted on the exhaust manifold, and on engine codes ACV, AUF, and AYC 2.5-litre units the compressed air is cooled by an intercooler mounted above the engine. Providing the engine has been serviced with regular oil changes, the turbocharger and associated parts should give very little trouble.

Exhaust system

The exhaust system fitted by the factory is probably the best for durability, and it is possible that diesel models are still running on the original system. A replacement exhaust from the catalytic converter back will more than likely be from an aftermarket manufacturer. This could be a cheap and cheerful system from a local tyre and exhaust outlet, or a state-of-the-art stainless steel unit tuned to achieve maximum power from the engine. Examine the exhaust system's entire length, paying particular attention to the silencer box end plates where condensation may result in corrosion. This is more relevant on the petrol-powered models. Also examine all the rubber mountings that suspend the system. Some – but not all – models are fitted with a catalytic converter; this should be examined closely, as it is an expensive item to replace. If you are looking at a big bore aftermarket exhaust, you may find during a test drive that it is very noisy, causing an irritating drone within the vehicle. Can you really stand that on a long road trip? Cheaper stainless steel systems may suffer from metal fatigue; this usually manifests itself as split or broken brackets that suspend the system.

If possible, check the entire length of the exhaust system, ends of the silencers, and tail pipe. An aftermarket dress-up tail pipe is featured here.

The bush in the gear change mechanism can wear, causing the rod to pop out (the bush is central in the pic with rust stains).

Transcription

All manual T4s have a five-speed gearbox, whereas the automatic box has four gears. A vibration when ticking over that stops when the clutch pedal is depressed is a sign that the dual-mass flywheel, fitted to 2.5-litre diesel engines, is past its best. A scream when the clutch pedal is depressed could be a worn clutch release bearing, while vibration when the clutch bites on taking off from rest could be a worn clutch pressure plate. This is not as noticeable on the models with the dual-mass flywheel, as this arrangement has a smoothing-out effect as the clutch bites. Noise apparent with the engine running and neutral selected could indicate worn input shaft bearings in the gearbox. Providing it is easy to select gears and the vehicle doesn't jump out of any gear, all is usually well. We would walk away and find a better example if we found a T4 that jumps out of gear, as this will prove to be an expensive repair. Gears that are difficult to engage could be due to worn linkage. In this case we recommend replacing the gear linkage bushes. The T4 with an automatic gearbox should shift gears smoothly and kick down to a lower gear to aid acceleration when the accelerator is depressed swiftly. On models with an automatic box produced before January 1993, a switch on the dashboard could be used to select sport mode; on later models this occurs automatically when a more aggressive driving style is detected. However, although the automatic allows a more relaxed driving style, they are noticeably heavier on fuel and very expensive to repair.

Syncro models

The running costs and reliability of the permanent four-wheel-drive syncro option compares favourably with other T4 models. The rear and front axles are connected

Syncro models with four-wheel-drive capabilities are desirable, but can be expensive to repair.

via a prop shaft through a viscous coupling; this can be expensive to rebuild, and the parts are becoming harder to find. The axle boots for the rear drive shafts are no longer available, but this can be overcome with generic over boots. Unfortunately, most syncro models we have seen for sale have a very high mileage, and good examples are hard to find. Problems associated with off-road use are not usually an issue, as – amazingly – most have never left the tarmac!

Brakes

The braking system used before May 1996 consists of a servo-assisted dual-circuit master cylinder, acting on discs at the front and self-adjusting drums at the rear. Thereafter, discs were fitted all round. A well-maintained T4 should have shiny discs and plenty of friction material left on the pads. The most likely problems occur on the rear discs, as these are subjected to the effects of more dirt from the road. A rusty rear disc may indicate a seized calliper, and in turn an inefficient handbrake.

The reservoir for the brake and clutch fluid is towards the rear of the engine compartment, and immediately forward of the driving position.

The front brake disc should be rust-free, devoid of deep grooves, and the brake pads evenly worn with sufficient material present.

From December 1990 until May 1996, self-adjusting drum brakes were fitted at the rear. Thereafter, all models were fitted with disc brakes all round.

Check the feel of the handbrake; any stiffness could be due to old and rusty cables, or a corroded handbrake mechanism on the rear callipers. This is not necessarily a walk-away problem if the rest of the T4 is up to standard; the repairs are fairly straightforward, and the parts relatively inexpensive.

Driveshafts

The driveshafts each have an inner and outer constant velocity joint protected by a rubber gaiter. A joint about to fail will click when cornering at low speed. Check the condition of the rubber gaiters, as a split gaiter will allow the ingress of dirt and grit, leading to joint failure.

Suspension and steering

The front suspension consists of upper and lower wishbones, with torsion bars connected to the upper wishbones to provide the suspension. Shock absorbers mounted between the lower wishbones and the subframe take care of the damping. An anti-roll bar is fitted between the two lower wishbones via a connecting link. The wishbones are mounted to the subframe with rubber bushes. The steering gear is a rack and pinion unit connected to the front stub axles with track-rods and ball joints. The front swivel hub is connected to the upper and lower wishbones with swivel ball joints, and houses the bearings for the drive shafts. The swivel ball joints are connected with a press fit into the wishbones. With the vehicle safely supported on axle stands, spin the front wheels to detect any noise or roughness in the wheel bearing. Grasp the road wheel top and bottom and try to rock it. Any movement found would be in the swivel ball joints, or possibly in the wheel bearing if roughness

The torsion bar suspension is connected to the upper wishbone. The photo shows the upper swivel joint, the trackrod end, and the steering rack.

The telescopic front shock absorber is connected to the lower wishbone. Check shock absorbers for fluid leakage.

The independent rear suspension consists of trailing arms, coil springs, and telescopic shock absorbers.

was detected. Also check the rubber gaiters on the ends of the steering rack; any splits or holes will allow the ingress of dirt and grit, causing premature wear in the steering rack.

The rear suspension consists of trailing arms and coil springs. If the coil springs are coil bound (compressed), they are likely to break, and should be replaced in pairs.

It is undoubtedly a popular ploy amongst enthusiasts to lower a T4. Apart from obvious ground clearance issues, this is likely to increase wear on suspension and steering components due to a change in the geometry, compared to the original factory specification.

Longevity

Provided the Transporter or Caravelle you are looking at has been well looked after, and repairs have been carried out as and when needed, the T4 – and especially the diesel models – can give very long service. Indeed, the internet forums are awash with claims boasting mileages well in excess of 200,000. Full-circle, the biggest enemy is corrosion, especially on neglected Buses and those living in, or subjected to, exposed coastal locations.

Test drive
Start checks

Before you test drive, check for play in the steering. With the steering in the straight-ahead position, attempt to move the steering wheel while watching the road wheel. If play is detected it could be in the lower wishbone swivel joint, trackrod end ball joints, or the outer ball joints in the steering rack. While stationary, also check the electrical equipment, lights, wipers, indicators, warning lights in the dashboard display, and the horn. As soon as the engine starts the oil pressure and alternator charging light should go out, and the handbrake warning light should only be on when the handbrake is engaged. A lack of water in the cooling system will cause another warning light to remain on.

Clutch and gearbox operation

Check how the clutch pedal feels; this is important, as there is a known problem with the bracket supporting it failing due to metal fatigue. It also gives the impression of a faulty clutch, as the reduced pedal movement causes the gears to crunch during changes. When moving off, the clutch should engage smoothly without juddering. A juddering clutch could be near the end of its useful life, or there might be oil contamination on the friction linings. A judder through the transmission when stationary could be due to a faulty dual-mass flywheel. When testing, drive hard through the gears to check that the vehicle doesn't jump out of gear. Don't forget to check reverse as well. The gears should engage smoothly unless the linkage is excessively worn.

Steering

The power-assisted steering should feel light and positive on the move. Any juddering through the steering wheel could be due to one or more wheels being out of balance.

Braking system

With disc brakes all around, the system gives confidence on the road. The mechanism on the rear brakes that operate the handbrake can seize, leading to a dead feel to the handbrake and a failure to hold the vehicle on a hill. This is a relatively common issue.

Noises

The hydraulic tappets may be noisy at start-up, but if the noise persists assume one or more tappets need replacement. This could also indicate a worn camshaft.

Worn front wheel bearings whine, but may be quieter during cornering when the bearing is under load, while worn rear wheel bearings usually give a low rumble.

If the constant velocity joints in the driveshafts click when cornering, they could be about to fail.

Oil pressure

The oil pressure light is the most important light concerning the health of the engine. If it comes on when driving, stop immediately and check the engine oil level.

Charging rate

As long as the alternator is charging the battery the warning light should remain off. If the warning light comes on while driving, stop and check the alternator drivebelt.

If the belt has broken you will be able to drive a short distance, as the cooling fan is electric and is controlled by a thermostatic switch.

Operation controls
All major controls are similar to most vehicles of the era.

Operation switches
The lights, heating and ventilation are controlled by rotary switches, while ancillaries such as a heated rear window and emergency flashers use rocker switches. The left-hand steering column stalk controls the direction indicators, headlight dip and main beam. The right-hand stalk controls the windscreen wipers. Switches for the electric cab windows are located on the door trim panels.

Ramp check
You may be able to arrange with a local garage or MOT station to lift the T4 on their ramp for a visual inspection of the underside. Look for corrosion in the under-body, paying particular attention to the sills and jacking points. Check the condition of the rubber gaiters on the driveshaft CV joints, and the rubber covers on all ball joints. Check the condition of the exhaust system, paying particular attention to the ends of the silencer boxes. Also examine the fixings holding it to the chassis. Examine the rubber brake pipes for cracking, and the metal pipes for corrosion. If possible, have an assistant in the driving seat to press the brake pedal, so that you can check the rubber brake hoses for bulging. Also have the assistant rock the steering to look for excessive movement in the steering components, such as lower swivel joints, trackrod ends and the ball joints in the ends of the steering rack. Check the engine and transmission for oil leaks, the radiator and hoses for water leaks, and any other suspicious fluid leaks.

Evaluation procedure
Add up the total points.
Score: 148 = excellent; 111 = good; 74 = average; 37 = poor. Cars scoring over 104 will be completely usable and will require only maintenance and care to preserve condition. Cars scoring between 37 and 75 will require some serious work (at much the same cost regardless of score). Cars scoring between 76 and 103 will require very careful assessment of the necessary repair/restoration costs in order to arrive at a realistic value.

10 Auctions
– sold! Another way to buy your dream

Auction pros & cons
Pros: Prices will usually be lower than those of dealers or private sellers and you might grab a real bargain on the day. Auctioneers have usually established clear title with the seller. At the venue you can usually examine documentation relating to the vehicle.
Cons: You have to rely on a sketchy catalogue description of condition & history. The opportunity to inspect is limited and you cannot drive the car. Auction cars are often a little below par and may require some work. It's easy to overbid. There will usually be a buyer's premium to pay in addition to the auction hammer price.

Which auction?
Auctions by established auctioneers are advertised in car magazines and on the auction houses' websites. A catalogue, or a simple printed list of the lots for auctions might only be available a day or two ahead, though often lots are listed and pictured on auctioneers' websites much earlier. Contact the auction company to ask if previous auction selling prices are available as this is useful information (details of past sales are often available on websites).

Catalogue, entry fee and payment details
When you purchase the catalogue of the vehicles in the auction, it often acts as a ticket allowing two people to attend the viewing days and the auction. Catalogue details tend to be comparatively brief, but will include information such as 'one owner from new, low mileage, full service history,' etc. It will also usually show a guide price to give you some idea of what to expect to pay and will tell you what is charged as a 'buyer's premium.' The catalogue will also contain details of acceptable forms of payment. At the fall of the hammer an immediate deposit is usually required, the balance payable within 24 hours. If the plan is to pay by cash there may be a cash limit. Some auctions will accept payment by debit card. Sometimes credit or charge cards are acceptable, but will often incur an extra charge. A bank draft or bank transfer will have to be arranged in advance with your own bank as well as with the auction house. No car will be released before all payments are cleared. If delays occur in payment transfers then storage costs can accrue.

Buyer's premium
A buyer's premium will be added to the hammer price: don't forget this in your calculations. It is not usual for there to be a further state tax or local tax on the purchase price and/or on the buyer's premium.

Viewing
In some instances it's possible to view on the day, or days before, as well as in the hours prior to, the auction. There are auction officials available who are willing to help out by opening engine and luggage compartments and to allow you to inspect the interior. While the officials may start the engine for you, a test drive is out of the question. Crawling under and around the car as much as you want is permitted, but

you can't suggest that the car you are interested in be jacked up, or attempt to do the job yourself. You can also ask to see any documentation available.

Bidding

Before you take part in the auction, decide your maximum bid – and stick to it! It may take a while for the auctioneer to reach the lot you are interested in, so use that time to observe how other bidders behave. When it's the turn of your car, attract the auctioneer's attention and make an early bid. The auctioneer will then look to you for a reaction every time another bid is made, usually the bids will be in fixed increments until the bidding slows, when smaller increments will often be accepted before the hammer falls. If you want to withdraw from the bidding, make sure the auctioneer understands your intentions – a vigorous shake of the head when he or she looks to you for the next bid should do the trick!

Assuming that you are the successful bidder, the auctioneer will note your card or paddle number, and from that moment on you will be responsible for the vehicle. If the car is unsold, either because it failed to reach the reserve or because there was little interest, it may be possible to negotiate with the owner, via the auctioneers, after the sale is over.

Successful bid

There are two more items to think about. How to get the car home, and insurance. If you can't drive the car, your own or a hired trailer is one way, another is to have the vehicle shipped using the facilities of a local company. The auction house will also have details of companies specialising in the transfer of cars.

Insurance for immediate cover can usually be purchased on site, but it may be more cost-effective to make arrangements with your own insurance company in advance, and then call to confirm the full details.

eBay & other online auctions?

eBay & other online auctions could land you a car at a bargain price, though you'd be foolhardy to bid without examining the car first, something most vendors encourage. A useful feature of eBay is that the geographical location of the car is shown, so you can narrow your choices to those within a realistic radius of home. Be prepared to be outbid in the last few moments of the auction. Remember, your bid is binding and that it will be very, very difficult to get restitution in the case of a crooked vendor fleecing you – caveat emptor!

Be aware that some cars offered for sale in online auctions are 'ghost' cars. Don't part with any cash without being sure that the vehicle does actually exist and is as described (usually pre-bidding inspection is possible).

Auctioneers

Barrett-Jackson www.barrett-jackson.com / **Bonhams** www.bonhams.com / **British Car Auctions (BCA)** www.bca-europe.com or www.british-car-auctions.co.uk / **Cheffins** www.cheffins.co.uk / **Christies** www.christies.com / **Coys** www.coys.co.uk / **eBay** www.eBay.com / **H&H** www.classic-auctions.co.uk / **RM** www.rmauctions.com / **Shannons** www.shannons.com.au / **Silver** www.silverauctions.com

11 Paperwork
– correct documentation is essential!

The paper trail

Classic, collector and prestige cars usually come with a large portfolio of paperwork accumulated and passed on by a succession of proud owners. This documentation represents the real history of the car, and from it can be deduced the level of care the car has received, how much it's been used, which specialists have worked on it and the dates of major repairs and restorations. All of this information will be priceless to you as the new owner, so be very wary of cars with little paperwork to support their claimed history.

Registration documents

All countries/states have some form of registration for private vehicles whether it's like the American 'pink slip' system or the British 'log book' system.

It is essential to check that the registration document is genuine, that it relates to the car in question, and that all the vehicle's details are correctly recorded, including chassis/VIN and engine numbers (if these are shown). If you are buying from the previous owner, his or her name and address will be recorded in the document: this will not be the case if you are buying from a dealer.

In the UK the current (Euro-aligned) registration document is the 'V5C,' and is printed in coloured sections of blue, green and pink. The blue section relates to the car specification, the green section has details of the new owner, and the pink section is sent to the DVLA in the UK when the car is sold. A small section in yellow deals with selling the car within the motor trade.

Previous ownership records

Due to the introduction of important new legislation on data protection, it is no longer possible to acquire, from the British DVLA, a list of previous owners of a car you own, or are intending to purchase. This scenario will also apply to dealerships and other specialists who you may wish to contact and acquire information on previous ownership and work carried out.

If the car has a foreign registration, there may be expensive and time-consuming formalities to complete. Do you really want the hassle?

Roadworthiness certificate

Most country/state administrations require that vehicles are regularly tested to prove they are safe to use on the public highway, and do not produce excessive emissions. In the UK that test (the 'MOT') is carried out at approved testing stations, for a fee. In the USA the requirement varies, but most states insist on an emissions test every two years as a minimum, while the police are charged with pulling over unsafe-looking vehicles.

In the UK the test is required on an annual basis once a vehicle becomes three years old. Of particular relevance for older cars is that the certificate issued includes the mileage reading at the test date and, therefore, becomes an independent record of that car's history. Ask the seller if previous certificates are available. Without an MOT the vehicle should be trailered to its new home, unless you insist that a valid MOT is part of the deal. (Not such a bad idea, this, as at least you will know the car was roadworthy on the day it was tested and you don't need to wait for the old certificate to expire before having the test done.)

In the UK, vehicles over 40 years old on May 20th each year, are exempt from MOT testing. Owners can still have the test carried out if they so wish.

Road licence

The administration of every country/state charges some kind of tax for the use of its road system, the actual form of the 'road licence' and, how it is displayed, varying enormously country to country and state to state.

Whatever the form of the 'road licence' it must relate to the vehicle carrying it, and must be present and valid if the car is to be driven on the public highway legally.

Changed legislation in the UK means that the seller of a car must surrender any existing road fund licence, and it is the responsibility of the new owner to re-tax the vehicle at the time of purchase and before the car can be driven on the road. It's therefore vital to see the Vehicle Registration Certificate (V5C) at the time of purchase, and to have access to the New Keeper Supplement (V5C/2), allowing the buyer to obtain road tax immediately.

In the UK, classic vehicles 40 years old or more, on the 1st January each year get free road tax. It is still necessary to renew the tax status every year, even if there is no change.

If the car is untaxed because it has not been used for a period of time, the owner has to inform the licensing authorities.

Certificates of authenticity

For many makes of collectible car it is possible to get a certificate proving the age and authenticity (eg engine and chassis numbers, paint colour and trim) of a particular vehicle, these are sometimes called 'Heritage Certificates' and if the car comes with one of these it is a definite bonus. If you want to obtain one, the relevant owners' club is the best starting point.

If the car has been used in European classic car rallies it may have a FIVA (Fédération International des Véhicules Anciens) certificate. The so-called 'FIVA Passport,' or 'FIVA Vehicle Identity Card,' enables organisers and participants to recognise whether or not a particular vehicle is suitable for individual events. If you want to obtain such a certificate go to www.fbhvc.co.uk or www.fiva.org. There will be similar organisations in other countries too.

Valuation certificate

Hopefully, the vendor will have a recent valuation certificate, or letter signed by a recognised expert stating how much he, or she, believes the particular car to be worth (such documents, together with photos, are usually needed to get 'agreed value' insurance). Generally such documents should act only as confirmation of your own assessment of the car rather than a guarantee of value as the expert has probably not seen the car in the flesh. The easiest way to find out how to obtain a formal valuation is to contact the owners' club.

Service history

Often these cars will have been serviced at home by enthusiastic (and hopefully capable) owners for a good number of years. Nevertheless, try to obtain as much service history and other paperwork pertaining to the car as you can. Naturally, dealer stamps, or specialist garage receipts score most points in the value stakes. However, anything helps in the great authenticity game, items like the original bill of sale, handbook, parts invoices and repair bills, adding to the story and the character of the car. Even a brochure correct to the year of the car's manufacture is a useful document and something that you could well have to search hard to locate in future years. If the seller claims that the car has been restored, then expect receipts and other evidence from a specialist restorer.

If the seller claims to have carried out regular servicing, ask what work was completed, when, and seek some evidence of it being carried out. Your assessment of the car's overall condition should tell you whether the seller's claims are genuine.

Restoration photographs

If the seller tells you that the car has been restored, then expect to be shown a series of photographs taken while the restoration was under way. Pictures taken at various stages, and from various angles, should help you gauge the thoroughness of the work. If you buy the car, ask if you can have all the photographs as they form an important part of the vehicle's history. It's surprising how many sellers are happy to part with their car and accept your cash, but want to hang on to their photographs! In the latter event, you may be able to persuade the vendor to get a set of copies made.

12 What's it worth?

– let your head rule your heart

Our message throughout is that there is no need to consider a rusty, battered T4. Indeed, we would strongly recommend you walk away from any such vehicle. Anything more than tiny bits of surface rust on, for example, the wheelarches that can be cosmetically rectified, and a T4 owner or enthusiast will tell you that the model you are looking at has been neglected over the years. Black moulded bumpers that look decidedly grey might offer another tell-tale sign, and unless before and after pictures are available to explain why a T4 has had a respray just before being put up for sale, there's another reason to be wary.

Once into the area of well-looked-after T4s, with service histories and possibly a tear in the seller's eye, our advice would be that unless you are mechanically adept, re-read the words of wisdom in earlier chapters, and then still have the Bus checked out by someone local who is in the know. If the vendor isn't keen on such a palaver, has he or she got something to hide?

Don't look at the body through rose-tinted spectacles; don't view on a wet day either. You will be overlooking what imperfections there are, or with your brolly or hood up, you simply won't be able to see them. Think about the expense associated with cosmetic panel re-sprays if you are really fussy, like one of the two of us. Even a scuffed colour-coded bumper is never cheap to make perfect. Find an alloy that has been scuffed and consider whether it will irritate you for years. Scrutinise the perfect upholstery with the exception of a worn driver's backrest. Can you turn a blind eye to that every time you climb into the cab?

Then there's the Camper angle. Has that interior been so well used that a tidy-up will be required sooner rather than later? Does a door or two drop on its hinges? Does everything work properly and, of course, is there evidence of a leaking elevating roof?

Let's be honest, even the best of T4s must have suffered a bit of normal wear and tear. A fastidious keeper will have rectified any dilapidation (okay, that's a bit over the top) as it becomes apparent. Perhaps the more average owner won't have, and it's then when you negotiate and when your head must rule your heart.

Oh, and if you are from a non-VW background, please remember that the T4 and many other models have a reputation for build-quality and sturdiness over gimmickry. For this reason, and due to the legions of VW fans, a good T4 is always likely to cost you more than an offering from a rival manufacturer.

13 Do you really want to restore?

– it'll take longer and cost more than you think

In a word: no! We've said all along that there are sufficient rock-solid, well-preserved T4s about to make it unnecessary. That said, there is an exception to the rule, as usual; more on that very shortly.

In the meantime, do you want to spend out? We hear wallets snapping shut the length and breadth of the country. Has your T4 got panels that have been resprayed at some time and don't quite match? Is the bonnet peppered with stone chips that, however cleverly touched-in by hand, are still irritatingly visible? Have you one or more alloys that over the years have developed a little corrosion? Have you got steel wheels and would like alloys? Have you bought a tin-top Camper, and would like the luxury of an elevating roof?

All of these factors, and others we simply haven't got space to list, cost money to deal with and cash that you won't completely recoup if you sell your T4. Should you be bothered? Well, in our opinion, definitely not. Try buying a brand new VW, or one that has been on the road for two or three years, and watch your money disappear at a rate of knots!

Therefore, we wouldn't restore, but we would take pride in our purchase.
This brings us neatly to the exception to the rule. How many of you achieve more

For sale at a show: slightly customised; well looked after. Here's ideal material to convert into a fully-fledged Camper.

Another option: buy a Delivery Van, add windows and seats, think about a colour scheme, personalise things like wheels, and purchase a big tent.

An example worthy of a feature article – luxury full camping interior, leather seats, T5 Toffee Brown paintwork, long-nose conversion from short, and a 140PS engine upgrade.

satisfaction working on your vehicles than driving them? How many of you want to create something bespoke to you? Yes, we thought so. Your aim, then, is to create your own T4 Camper, possibly your own people carrier, or weekender and bike carrier combined.

Under such circumstances, what you are really looking for is either a good, sound Delivery Van, or a Kombi (as the name implies a combination of seating and goods storage), or a similar vehicle referred to by VW as a Window Van.

Here, as usual, we don't want rust, and there is no need to consider mechanical failure, but wear and tear is both inevitable and acceptable. Odds-on that you will respray your new pride and joy – you may well have taken the can opener to a Delivery Van's panels to add windows. In all probability you'll put some posh wheels on your T4, you may opt to lower it, you might even put a long-nose front on a short-nose van – we've seen it done. Inside, you'll probably rip out just about everything. Captain's chairs could well replace VW's originals, you might opt to flock the dash, and inevitably bare metal won't be a feature of the rear area. Insert a kit (we know one owner who did that on his driveway), build your own, or farm it out to the professionals.

What you are doing isn't restoration, as such, but is as near as we would recommend.

www.velocebooks.com / www.veloce.co.uk
Details of all current books • New book news • Special offers

14 Paint problems
– bad complexion, including dimples, pimples and bubbles

Paint faults generally occur due to lack of protection/maintenance, or because of poor preparation prior to a respray or touch-up. Some of the following conditions may be present in the car you're looking at:

Orange peel
This appears as an uneven paint surface, similar to the skin of an orange. The fault is caused by the failure of atomised paint droplets to flow into each other when they hit the surface. It's sometimes possible to rub out the effect with proprietary paint cutting/rubbing compound or very fine grades of abrasive paper. A respray may be necessary in severe cases. Consult a bodywork repairer/paint shop for advice on the particular car.

Cracking
Severe cases are likely to have been caused by too heavy an application of paint (or filler beneath the paint). Also, insufficient stirring of the paint before application can lead to the components being improperly mixed, and cracking can result. Incompatibility with the paint already on the panel can have a similar effect. To rectify the problem it is necessary to rub down to a smooth, sound finish before respraying the problem area.

Don't be tempted, whatever the bargain price. There are so many T4s about that need little or no work doing to the paint.

Dull – not the Double Chassis Cab, but the paint. A good going-over with T-Cut (or similar) should cure most of the ills.

Paint looks good, but the bumpers are scuffed and faded. There's always the option to paint them ... standard on higher specification T4s.

Crazing
Sometimes the paint takes on a crazed rather than a cracked appearance when the problems mentioned under 'Cracking' are present. This problem can also be caused by a reaction between the underlying surface and the paint. Paint removal and respraying the problem area is usually the only solution.

Blistering
Almost always caused by corrosion of the metal beneath the paint. Usually perforation will be found in the metal and the damage will usually be worse than that suggested by the area of blistering. The metal will have to be repaired before repainting.

Micro blistering
Usually the result of an economy respray where inadequate heating has allowed moisture to settle on the car before spraying. Consult a paint specialist, but usually damaged paint will have to be removed before partial or full respraying. Can also be caused by car covers that don't 'breathe.'

Fading
Some colours, especially reds, are prone to fading if subjected to strong sunlight for long periods without the benefit of polish protection. Sometimes proprietary paint restorers and/or paint cutting/rubbing compounds will retrieve the situation. Often a respray is the only real solution.

Smart T4, but removing graphics can often leave a ghost of the lettering, which the pernickety would think demanded repainting. Think discount, perhaps?

Ex-AA vans are usually mechanically good, and therefore worth investing in a decent splash of paint for to change their identity.

A full respray/change of colour could hide accident damage or evidence of the tin worm ... always worth checking.

Peeling

Often a problem with metallic paintwork when the sealing lacquer becomes damaged and begins to peel off. Poorly applied paint may also peel. The remedy is to strip and start again!

Dimples

Dimples in the paintwork are caused by the residue of polish (particularly silicone types) not being removed properly before respraying. Paint removal and repainting is the only solution.

Dents

Small dents are usually easily cured by the 'Dentmaster,' or equivalent process, that sucks or pushes out the dent (as long as the paint surface is still intact). Companies offering dent removal services usually come to your home: consult your telephone directory.

15 Problems due to lack of use

– just like their owners, T4s need exercise!

Cars, like humans, are at their most efficient if they exercise regularly. A run of at least ten miles, once a week, is recommended for classics.

Seized components
Pistons in callipers, slave and master cylinders can seize.
The clutch may seize if the plate becomes stuck to the flywheel because of corrosion.
Handbrakes (parking brakes) can seize if the cables and linkages rust.
Pistons can seize in the bores due to corrosion.

Fluids
Old, acidic, oil can corrode bearings.
Uninhibited coolant can corrode internal waterways. Lack of antifreeze can cause core plugs to be pushed out, even cracks in the block or head. Silt settling and solidifying can cause overheating.
Brake fluid absorbs water from the atmosphere and should be renewed every two years. Old fluid with a high water content can cause corrosion and pistons/calipers to seize (freeze), and can cause brake failure when the water turns to vapor near hot braking components.

Rust can form on the brake discs (or drums on older models), eventually causing them to seize solid.

If a T4 has been left standing for a long time, the tyres develop flat spots. Safety, if nothing else, demands they are changed immediately.

The rubber trim has become dislodged, allowing ingress of water and the inevitable outbreak of rust – easily avoidable with regular maintenance.

Tyre problems
Tyres that have had the weight of the car on them in a single position for some time will develop flat spots, resulting in some (usually temporary) vibration. The tyre walls may have cracks or (blister-type) bulges, meaning new tyres are needed.

Shock absorbers (dampers)
With lack of use, the dampers will lose their elasticity or even seize. Creaking, groaning and stiff suspension are signs of this problem.

Rubber and plastic
Radiator hoses may have perished and split, possibly resulting in the loss of all coolant. Window and door seals can harden and leak. Gaitors/boots can crack. Wiper blades will harden.

Electrics
The battery will be of little use if it has not been charged for many months. Earthing/grounding problems are common when the connections have corroded. Old bullet and spade type electrical connectors commonly rust/corrode, and will need disconnecting, cleaning and protection (eg Vaseline). Sparkplug electrodes will often have corroded in an unused engine. Wiring insulation can harden and fail.

Rotting exhaust system
Exhaust gas contains a high water content, so exhaust systems corrode very quickly from the inside when the car is not used.

16 The Community

– key people, organisations and companies in the T4 world

Clubs across the world

Australia

Club Vee Dub Sydney
www.clubvw.org.au

Volkswagen Club Victoria
www.vwclub.com.au

Germany

All-VW-Club Niederflur
www.niederflur.de

South Africa

VW Club of South Africa
www.vwclub.co.za

United Kingdom

Volkswagen Owners' club (Great Britain)
C/o PO Box 7, Burntwood, Staffs
WS7 2SB.
Tel: 01952 242167
www.vwocgb.com
The oldest VW club in Britain. Caters for all models whether water-cooled or air-cooled.

www.vwt4forum.co.uk
(online forum and club)

www.t4club.co.uk
(online forum and club)

www.just-t4s.co.uk
(online forum and club)

USA

For a list of clubs visit:
www.hubcapcafe.com/resources/
volkswagen_clubs.htm

Specialists

There are so many businesses specialising in T4 parts, tuning, conversions and sales that we have restricted our listing to UK only. This list does not imply recommendation and is not deemed to be comprehensive. We've included two garages that have been helpful in the compilation of this book.

Heritage Parts Centre (Parts supplier)
47 Dolphin Road, Shoreham-By-Sea
West Sussex
BN43 6PB
Tel: 01273 44 40 00
Email: help@heritagepartscentre.com
www.vwheritage.com

Just Kampers (Parts supplier)
Unit 1, Stapeley Manor
Long Lane, Odiham
Hampshire
RG29 1JE
Tel: 0345 121 5656
www.justkampers.com

German Swedish & French (Parts supplier)
Branches all over the country
Mail Order Tel: 020 8917 3866
www.gsfcarparts.com

Euro Car Parts (Parts supplier)
Branches nationwide
Tel: 0870 150 6506
www.eurocarparts.com

Hulins (Repairs and spares)
Tel: 01452 502333 (Gloucester)

Calverley Autos (Repairs)
Craig Johnson (Leeds/Bradford area)
Tel: 0113 255 8639

Votex (Service, repairs and Tuning)
West Street, Congleton
Cheshire
CW12 1JR
Tel: 01260 29 75 79

Email: contact@votex.ltd.uk
www.votex.ltd.uk

EVO Design (specialist flat-pack
furniture, parts & kits)
6 Westminster Road, Wareham
Dorset
BH20 4SP
Tel: 01929 55 00 00
Email: evomotiondesign@gmail.com
www.evomotiondesign.co.uk

Jack's Shack (Camper conversions)
90 Islington Street, Freemens Common
Leicester
LE2 7SQ
Tel: 01162 55 50 81
Email: jack@jacks-shack.co
www.jacks-shack.co

CJC Vans (Camper conversions)
Unit 11, Three Springs Industrial Estate
Worcester
WR5 1BW
Tel: 01905 35 86 71
Mobile: 07985 268 121
Email: info@cjcvans.co.uk
www.cjcvans.co.uk

Eclipse Custom Campers
(Camper conversions)
9B Oxford Road
Pen Mill Trading Estate
Yeovil
BA21 5HR
Tel: 01935 32 15 64
Mobile: 07760 888 916
Email: info@eclipsecampers.com
www.eclipsecampers.com

T4 T5 Transformations
(Camper conversions)
2 Manor Row, Wakefield
Yorkshire
WF2 8DD
Tel: 01924 33 90 04
Mobile: 07840 377 387
Email: info@notjustcampers.com
www.notjustcampers.com

Westdubs (Elevating Roof)
Unit 4D, 4E, 4F
Bruff Business Centre
Suckley
Worcestershire
WR6 5DR
Tel: 01886 88 45 55
Email: t5vw@live.co.uk
www.westdubs.co.uk

Low-life Products Ltd (Elevating Roof)
The Wharf Garage, Grimshaw Lane
Bollington
Cheshire
SK10 5JB
Tel: 01625 70 74 01

HiLo (Elevating Roof)
www.hiloroofs.co.uk

Evesham Auto Spares
(specialist VW Transporter salvage)
Tel: 01386 83 11 02
Mobile: 07483 12 58 33
Email: eveshamautospares@gmail.com
www.volkswagenspares.com

Volks-Apart (VW salvage)
Unit 1 Burnett Road
Darent Industrial Park
Erith
Greater London
Tel: 020 8309 6200

Stevens VW Dismantlers (VW salvage)
Chelmsford, Essex
Tel: 01245 362020
www.vws.me.uk

Book
*Volkswagen T4 – Transporter, Caravelle,
Multivan, Camper and EuroVan 1990 –
2003*, Richard Copping, The Crowood
Press ISBN 978 1 84797-554-6

17 Vital statistics
– essential data at your fingertips

Short-nose, long-nose, pre- and post-revamped bumpers ... here's the smallest and biggest T4 found.

Short wheelbase, short-nose, circa 1990
Length: 4655mm; width: 1840mm; height: 1940mm (note – there is a short-nose, high-roof van, height: 2430mm, but only available with a long-wheelbase).

Long-wheelbase, long-nose, circa 1996
Length: 5189mm; width: 1840mm; height: 1940mm (note – a few Campers may be based on the SWB version of the long-nose, as is the Multivan, length: 4789mm).

Numerous engines were offered. The spec given is that of the 2.5TDI recommended as a first option throughout the guide.

Engine
Front-mounted, transverse, water-cooled, five-cylinder, in-line, with turbocharger and intercooler.
Capacity: 2459cc
Max power: 102PS @ 3500rpm
Max torque: 250Nm @ 1900-2300rpm
Bore and stroke: 81.0x95.5mm
Compression ratio: 19.5:1
Exhaust system: Oxidation catalytic converter and exhaust recirculation
Fuel system: Electronically-controlled direct injection
Tank capacity: 80 litres (17.6 gallons)
Max speed: 98mph
Consumption (mpg):
 Urban cycle: 34.9
 Constant 56mph: 43.5
 Constant 75mph: 30.7

Brakes
Dual-circuit hydraulic split front/rear with servo assistance – front and rear disc brakes.

Wheels
6J x 15 steel wheels with 205/65R15 C tyres (alloys optional).

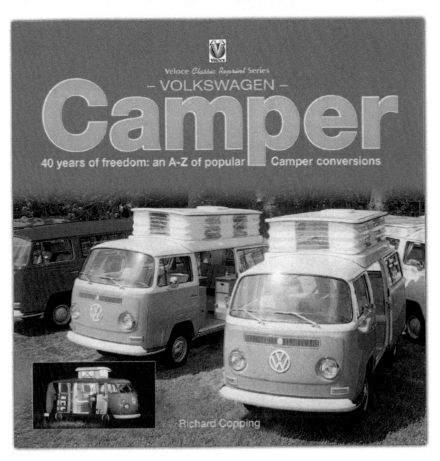

Volkswagen Camper
40 years of freedom: an A-Z of popular Camper conversions

Back in print after a long absence!
Delving exclusively into the spin-off conversions based on the VW Panelvan, Kombi and Microbus. Designed in the style of the original VW sales literature, this book tells the complete story of the Volkswagen-based Camper phenomenon, written by a knowledgeable enthusiast.

ISBN: 978-1-787111-22-6
Paperback • 22.5x22.5cm • 176 pages • 182 colour and b&w pictures

For more information and price details, visit our website at www.veloce.co.uk
• email: info@veloce.co.uk • Tel: +44(0)1305 260068

The Essential Buyer's Guide™ series ...

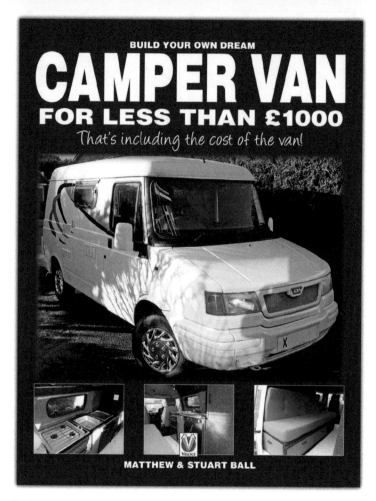

Build Your Own Dream Camper Van for less than £1000

You can build your own dream campervan in just ten weeks – for less than £1000! This book gives easy, step-by-step illustrated instructions for the amateur DIYer on a budget. Full of original money- and time-saving ideas, such as how to kit out your interior for free, and source your van for peanuts. The ideas in this book will work on any van.

ISBN: 978-1-845845-24-7
Paperback • 27x20.7cm • 128 pages • 287 pictures

For more information and price details, visit our website at www.veloce.co.uk
• email: info@veloce.co.uk • Tel: +44(0)1305 260068

Index

Notes

9781787114388